Tuning In to Family Destiny

Passing on Family Potential to Future Generations

The Story of Joe Clemmer
Mennonite Music and Worship Pioneer

*by Wesley Clemmer
& Janet Clemmer Zeager*

Tuning In to Family Destiny
Passing on Family Potential to Future Generations

THE STORY OF JOE CLEMMER

MENNONITE MUSIC AND
WORSHIP PIONEER

© 2009 by Wes Clemmer

Library of Congress Number: 2009905779
ISBN: 978-1-60126-186-1

Masthof Press
*219 Mill Road
Morgantown, PA 19543-9516
www.masthof.com*

Contents

Acknowledgements v
Foreword vii
Introduction xi

1. Birthing of the Vision 1
2. Dad's Roots 5
3. Formative Foundations 11
4. Trauma, Trials and Training 19
5. Pass It On 33
6. The Franconia Frustration 39
7. Straddling the Fence 43
8. Mom's Roots 47
9. Edie My Sweetie 53
10. Sound of the Islands 60
11. Family Callings 67
12. Pioneering Prayer 73
13. A Heart for Family 78
14. The Macedonian Call 86
15. Peer Pioneers 94
16. The Test of Fellowship 101
17. The Rich Routines of Home 110
18. On the Lawn 121
19. Concert Expansion 127
20. Providential Partners 131
21. Music-Man Merchandising 140

22. Inspiration and Reproduction 145
23. Note-Worthy Trips 155
24. Evolution of the Clemmer Sound 164
25. For the Record 170
26. Northland Pioneer Adventure 176
27. Celt Lake Crisis.. 185
28. The Business Boom 193
29. Extending and Ending 199
30. Sunset Years... 204
31. Blessings and Offerings 208

Epilogue: *Tuning in to Family Destiny*............................... 216

Appendix I: *Creating a Memorial Stone* 221
Appendix II: *Legacy Letter* 224
Appendix III: *Chord Chart and Theme Song*................... 229

Acknowledgements

We want to express gratitude for the many friends and family members who have made such valuable contributions to this project.

First, we desire to thank you, Verna and Charlie, for the many ways you have encouraged and assisted us. Without your daily support and countless sacrifices this book would not have been written. You are wonderful spouses.

Lucy and Dean—you have shared front-row seats with us in the real-life drama of our parents. That investment is vital. You, along with your spouses have helped us in many different ways to put this story together. We are deeply grateful.

Brothers and sisters of Dad and Mom—we take this opportunity to bless you for the special part each of you have played in blessing our parents throughout their entire lives. Special thanks to Jake, Marvin, Alice, Betty and Martha for giving us a better understanding of those growing up years. We were not present for that part of the story!

Interviews in person, by phone, and email have been a wonderful benefit as well. It has been a joy to interact personally with you—Earl Alderfer, Bill and Miriam Anders, Verna Bechtel, Irene Deiter, Gerald Derstine, Naomi Hackman (wife of Floyd), Wayne Martin, and Marlene Styer. Dad and Mom loved each of you very much. Your part in their story is more significant than you can ever know.

"Big John" Bechtel, what a delight to hear from you again. And the story about retuning your guitar between lessons with Dad—what an amusing tidbit.

We would have missed a vital ingredient had I [Wes] not been privileged to interact with church and community historian, John Ruth. Thank you, John, for the priceless investment you have made through the years to preserve so much of our history. I'm also grateful for the copy of your video interview with Dad. It is another lasting tribute to his life and ministry in music.

Michael and Jane Bailey—reading the manuscript, providing editorial assistance, probing, prodding and priming the pump of creativity . . . you both are a true gift.

And, to all the countless partners of divine providence, named and unnamed, who crossed Dad and Mom's path and contributed in some way to their story—without you, there would be no story!

Foreword

Lives well lived are monuments for future generations. A monument is defined as "a lasting evidence or reminder of someone notable—a memorial stone erected in remembrance of a person."

God places great importance on preserving memories for future generations. After the children of Israel crossed the Jordan River on dry ground, God instructed Joshua, their leader, to construct a monument. Choosing one man from each tribe, these leaders were to gather rocks from the middle of the river. This mound of stones was constructed as a memorial, providing witness to future generations of God's mighty hand in parting the waters.

> *"Let this be a sign among you, so that when your children ask later, saying, 'What do these stones mean to you?' then you shall say to them, 'Because the waters of the Jordan were cut off before the ark of the covenant of the Lord; when it crossed the Jordan, the waters of the Jordan were cut off.' So these stones shall become a memorial to the sons of Israel forever."*
> Joshua 4:6, 7

It has been said that "to understand a man or woman you must understand their memories." Today's experiences are producing tomorrow's memories. My children and grandchildren often hear me say, "We made a memory today!"

As my brother, Wes, and I began working on this project, we started searching through Dad and Mom's memories. In the process, hidden treasures were uncovered that helped us become better acquainted with them. These memories, many previously hidden, took us deeper in a more intimate way. The details and experiences of their lives began unfolding in a delightful fashion. Delving into their fascinating backgrounds and weaving heritage and life experiences together revealed the vivid mosaic of their colorful lives.

This is a story about two common people who allowed God to use them in uncommon ways. Dad's pioneering spirit blended with Mother's faithful support, producing a lovely tapestry for the glory of God.

Herein is a story of love, courage, faithfulness, and deep commitment, fleshed out amid the joys and struggles of life. Called to engage in unusual exploits, they advanced God's purposes and in so doing brought blessings to countless people. After Mom went home to be with the Lord, I found the following poem in her Bible. It accurately describes her journey with Dad on this earth:

> *Lord, help me live from day to day*
> *In such a self-forgetful way,*
> *That even when I kneel to pray*
> *My prayer shall be for 'Others.'*
>
> *Help me in all the work I do*
> *To ever be sincere and true,*
> *And know that all I do for You*
> *Must needs be done for 'Others.'*
>
> *And when my work on earth is done*
> *And my new work in Heaven's begun,*
> *May I forget the crown I've won*
> *While thinking still of 'Others.'*
>
> *Others, Lord, yes, Others!*
> *Let this my motto be,*
> *Help me to live for others*
> *That I may live for Thee.*

It has been a joy to witness Mom and Dad's love for God, for each other, and for those they touched. I feel greatly blessed to be part of their story firsthand for so many years. My parents are heroes and role models, having imparted a priceless legacy to me through their meaningful lives.

My prayer and desire is that Dad and Mom's story will help my children, grandchildren, and future generations know who they are by learning where they came from.

Another goal is that you, the reader, will be touched and challenged by the exemplary lives of my parents. May this story inspire you to pursue God's destiny for your life. As you catch the spark of their venturesome, enthusiastic spirit, may their obedience to God ignite a burning desire in your heart to follow in their footsteps.

That is why we share Dad and Mom's life and experiences with you through this written word—a memorial stone that can be held close to the heart and inspire over and over again.

- Janet Clemmer Zeager

Introduction

Human beings are truly amazing. As word-based creatures, we are the only one of our kind. Word language is unique to us as humans. Roses communicate beauty by producing a fragrance. Birds interact with one another by the uniqueness of their melodic songs. Sunsets declare the glory of God, showcasing the glow of their pink and purple hues. But we, the crowning glory of God's creation, use words. It is because we are created in His likeness—in the image of the God who is, at His creative best, The Word.

Through the use of words I express my humanity. I speak words. I write words. When I converse with words, you can begin to know who I am. If you choose to hear and to respond, word exchange begins. The ongoing interchange of words becomes language. We speak. We listen. We lean forward, intent to understand. Without understanding, language deteriorates. Words become mere words. Though we continue to communicate, we fail to connect. We lose touch. We miss out on the interchange of life.

Story is vital to language and life. It helps us to understand. God knows this principle well. That's why He uses stories so much. In fact that's what all of history represents. His-Story. It's what we are about. Almost everyone enjoys a story. I can vividly recall a recent time when I had just completed reading a story to my four-year-old granddaughter. I had barely uttered the last word, when out of her mouth came, "Read the story again, Grandpa!"

Stories can be about an endless number of things, but most stories involve people. I personally believe the most interesting and enlightening stories are about real people. This could be because every person is uniquely different. Humans have much in common with one another. But when it comes to being me, I am radically unlike any other person living before or after me. The same is true of you. Each of us is unique—a never-to-be-duplicated work of God's artistry.

This being the case, every people-story is unique in timing, in content, in value. For the generations gone before us, their earthly story has concluded. Yes, there is more to be written in the eternal sense, but this first book of their "grand story" is now history.

For those of us still living, our story is in process—still being created. Some of us are near the closing chapters; others closer to the beginning. For many, your story seems to have little rhyme or reason. Others appear to have more of a flow. Certain ones have a good bit of drama. Some seem to be rather uneventful. But hold on. There's more to the story.

* * *

Written histories of people are valuable. They connect us with those who have laid foundations we are called to build upon. Through the gift of words and language and story, we are enriched with the privilege of knowing people even though we never knew them. Yes, there are some obvious limitations to knowing a person only though a historical account, but story helps—tremendously. As with puzzles, each piece has a purpose. Eugene Peterson, in his book *Five Smooth Stones*, helps us understand this truth.

> "*The Hebrews were the world's first historians. Because they were convinced that God worked among them where they were, each day, they believed that what they did, whether in faith or unbelief, sin or righteousness, obedience or rebellion, was significant. Because it was significant, it was capable of being narrated as a story. That is, as an account in which what people did had consequences and was part of a structured pur-*

pose. *A story begins, has a middle, and ends. Everything in it has a point, a meaning. Nothing is irrelevant. Each character, however minor, plays a part.*"

I recall reading this paragraph many years ago, and underlining it. I made a mental note, thinking of how important it was to preserve life-stories. They are easily lost if not intentionally recorded. I can't recall thinking about Dad's story at the time, but somewhere along the way I made that connection. Dad was living at the time. Today, he's not living . . . here.

Dad was a great storyteller! People enjoyed listening to his stories, and he had many. Most storytellers do. I can recall times when I got a bit tired of hearing his stories, over and over again. But ironically, I find myself, after all these years, still telling some of his "boring" stories. Even though remembering many of his stories because of hearing them so often, I began realizing much of his personal story would be lost if not intentionally written down. The longer I pondered this possibility, the more sober I became. Though having personally walked through most of Dad's story with him, I realized that, over time, I would forget much of it. I also knew there were portions I had never heard.

If this was true for me, what about my children and grandchildren? How much would they miss by not having "the rest of the story?" What about those beyond our immediate family who never knew Dad, or possibly only knew him from a distance? I was coming to realize what a treasure his story represents.

As I pondered all of this, it was as if a wave of inspiration washed over me. A written legacy could actually extend Dad's influence beyond his lifetime. If I could enlist his help and write his story, it could be said of Dad as is recorded in the scriptures of Abel: "Though he is dead, he still speaks." It was with this conviction that I sat down at my computer [seventeen years ago] and composed a letter and sent it to Dad. Though written for him, I don't think he would mind me sharing that "legacy letter" with you [see Appendix II].

I'm happy to report that Dad took my letter to heart. He and Mom did just as I had requested. As they began recording story entries in their notebook, it became apparent how difficult it was for Dad to tell his own story. Most entries were just a few short paragraphs; generally factual. Much of what would provide great interest—feelings, heart-talk, struggles, elations—was missing. Fortunately, in the process of our story-writing project, significant dimensions of the inner story have been revealed.

Dad only lived four more years after I first solicited his help. During that time Dad's health deteriorated quite rapidly. How I wish I had initiated this mission years earlier.

In portions of the story, Jan and I have taken liberty to create dialog that is not word for word as it actually happened. We have prayerfully labored over these interpretations, seeking to reflect the spirit of what actually took place in each encounter. The sprinkling of dialog, like food seasonings, will help to bring out the flavor of the story. Again, we want you to experience this book as a storybook, not a history book.

Well, enough talk about the story. Let's get on with it. But don't forget. Destiny is the reason for the story!

- Wesley A. Clemmer

1

Birthing of the Vision

The evening stillness had settled once again upon the rolling hills of the picturesque Indian Valley. Barn chores were completed. The lingering sounds of suppertime cleanup in the large farm kitchen had given way to the buzz of family conversation in the front parlor. Now, only an occasional creak from a rope bed gave evidence to the fact that one or two members of this energetic family had not yet fallen off to sleep.

From the other side of the house, another sound drifted up the darkened front-hall staircase to join those creaks in the bedroom. It was a haunting sound; somewhat melodious, but with a touch of raw emotion. A lone kerosene lantern in the front-room parlor revealed a man. His hands moved almost effortlessly as he commanded sounds from the strings of a well-worn guitar. The rhythmic strum of his right hand would occasionally be interrupted by a single-string run, all in keeping with the familiar strains of "The Wreck of the Old Ninety-Seven." The musician's throaty voice, worn by years of use, added lyrics to his tune.

The cowboy was not alone. A young, lanky lad sat crouched by the doorway out in the dark hallway. He lingered, mesmerized by this intriguing sound filtering through the closed parlor door. The lad shivered in the cold darkness, automatically pulling up the collar of his gray flannel overcoat in a fleeting attempt to keep warm. His body, wearied by a hard day's work of barn chores and school learning, cried out for its due rest. But there was a deeper cry being birthed in the inner recesses of his soul.

That sound. There was nothing like it. It held him captive. Quietly, Dad shifted himself and leaned forward with his ear against the door. He visualized the cowboy's left hand, imagining the quick movements of fingers forming and re-forming each harmonious chord. How did he do it? How could he remember? What a mystery. The melody sounded almost heavenly. Dad found himself lost in a flood of questions and feelings that bombarded both mind and soul.

The music suddenly stopped, quickly breaking the mood of the moment. "Guess I needa quit," Gotshall yawned under his breath. Dad's heart cried out, silently petitioning, "Once more!" As if in response to a soundless messenger transmitting this plea, Gotshall strummed a C chord, paused briefly to retune the E string, and immediately launched into an encore of the same old tune.

It was a golden moment. Dad was drawing life from that sound. It seemed to touch every fiber of his being. Oh that it would never end. Morning would be here all too quickly. With the dawn would come daily chores and the farm life he had come to know all too well. If only he had been fortunate enough to be born into a different family, in a different place, at a different time. There would be no greater joy on the face of this earth then to create music just like Gotshall. Was that really an impossible wish?

Tiptoeing up the steps on the way to his room, Dad found himself breathing a petition to the Lord. As he slipped into bed, Dad's body welcomed the prospects of rest, but his mind was running fast. Maybe, just maybe, he could convince Pop to buy him a guitar. No, that would be unheard of. Work, work, work was all Pop knew. He seemed to be unmoved by Gotshall's guitar picking. And besides, money was tight and times were tough. Pop had just mentioned yesterday about needing to replace the plow. What would be the use of even mentioning the guitar?

Dad listened to the even breathing of Jake as he lay next to him. His mind mentally pictured each of his other brothers and sisters. Why could he not treat this guitar music like the rest of his family, in the same casual way? Was he crazy? Why could he not just listen and go on living life? Sleep came, but it was far from peaceful. These were valid questions but without rational answers—questions needing to be asked and answered another day.

* * *

It was a mile walk to school. Jake and Cyrus were halfway out the long farm lane as Dad grabbed his coat and hurried out the door. Mum had delayed him with one last-minute kitchen chore, and he needed to make tracks. Dad's thoughts rambled as he settled into an aggressive gait that would eventually catch his brothers.

Secretly, Dad was kinda glad for the graying skies that held the promise of a reprieve from busy fall farm work. Not that farming was without its joys. He could vividly recall the exhausting satisfaction of finishing the large field of corn husking just a few weeks earlier. A lingering sense of fulfillment remained. His hands and back had invested their strength to help reap the bountiful harvest that was now filling the barn and corn crib. But life was more than farming. Something had changed ever since the guitar-pickin' tenant had moved in on the other side of their sprawling farmhouse.

Walter Gotshall had been a hometown guy. But, with a wandering spirit and unquenchable desire for faraway places, Walter had packed his bags and headed west. Montana ended up being his destination. After experiencing his fill of cowboy life, Gotshall said good-by to the open plains of the Wild West. He found himself headed back east, back home to Harleysville. Acquainted with the Clemmer family, he had heard of Pop looking for a tenant to rent the vacant half of their farmhouse. Gotshall contacted Pop and made the necessary arrangements.

As Dad tuned in to the sounds of Walter's nightly guitar-pickin' sessions, a new stirring began down deep in his soul. It overshadowed the allure of competing in those checker games with Pop or his brothers at the kitchen table. It surpassed the fun of ball games with school chums. There was something unexplainable about Walter's cowboy music. And the longer Dad listened, the less content he was with just listening.

"I'm gonna learn for myself," Dad muttered under his breath as he finally got within a few strides of his brothers. Together they broke into a full-out run as the school bell announced the start of a typical school day. Daydreams of guitars and cowboy tunes would have to give way to more mundane things like books and studying. But, this brewing passion for learning to pick guitar was not about to be aborted. Something was being birthed that would have amazed this lanky twelve-year-old lad and his schoolteacher that chilly November day. This birthing would have also astounded Mum, the one chosen by God to mother Dad in natural birth.

2

Dad's Roots

The early morning sun cast shadows across the lane as Alice, great with child, trudged up the stone walk to her simple farmhouse. This large dwelling was her birthplace. It had been in her family for generations.

Spring flowers were in full bloom. Trees were bursting forth with fresh green foliage. The farmland was in a heavy state of cultivation. Fields were plowed. Blue bells dressed the meadow, their blue hue radiating amid the lush grass and clover. A squirrel scampered up the old gnarled maple tree in the front yard. New life was evident all around on this twenty-third day of May. New life was also stirring in this attractive young mother.

Alice had been experiencing slight birth pangs for several hours. They had awakened her before the early morning dawn. As hours passed, the pains increased. Would this be a boy or a girl she wondered, welcoming the rest between contractions.

Just then, Allen came into the house from the apple orchard and asked Alice how she was feeling. "I think you'd better call Doc Keeler," she said, doubling over with a strong contraction. Allen hurried to the party-line phone. He was anxious to have Doc on hand in time for the delivery of their new baby.

Alice's mother appeared from the other side of the house to help with preparations. She stirred the ashes in the stove, added a few pieces of wood, and then went outside to the water pump. Bustling back into the kitchen, she began heating the water and gathering some old bed sheets.

Confident that her mother had things under control, Alice laboriously climbed the stairs to her rope bed. She wasn't there long until she heard her mother greeting Doc Keeler as he arrived in his horse and wagon. Doc came into their bedroom toting his well-worn black bag. After a few labored hours, strong cries from the newborn baby echoed throughout the house.

"It's a boy!" Allen exclaimed as he gazed at the wiggling infant. "Jake will have a brother to play with," Alice murmured. Allen was glad for another son to eventually help with the never-ending farm work. Alice's mother washed the newborn baby and swaddled him in a warm blanket. As she placed the infant in his mother's welcoming arms, Alice tenderly grasped his tiny hand and pressed it to her mouth. Before the birth, she had bits of interaction with this precious baby. Now she could begin enjoying the full reward of intimate face-to-face relationship. What kind of personality would he have? What would this son do in life? Might he someday take over the family farm?

"What are you going to name him?" the doctor asked, interrupting her rambling thoughts. "His name will be Joseph, named after my brother," Alice announced. Her brother, Joe Moyer, was a mail carrier between Souderton, Telford, and Vernfield. He had a hearty sense of humor acquired from his father, William Moyer. Joe was a very pleasant man and easy to talk to. People were drawn to him and enjoyed his friendship. "Yes," Allen added. "His name will be Joseph Eugene." And so it was that on this beautiful spring day, Allen and Alice were blessed with a precious gift from God—another son to raise for His honor and glory.

When Dad was born he already had a brother, Jake, who was two years older. Close in age, they were bound to share countless boyhood experiences, growing up together on the farm. Other siblings were to follow.

* * *

Three years after Dad's birth, Bill was born. Cyrus came two years later, expanding the family circle. Alice was kept busy with her four active boys. She was happy for Pop, knowing the great help these sons

Allen Landis Clemmer (1890-1967) and Alice Moyer Clemmer (1893-1986) father and mother of Joe Clemmer. The great-grandmother of Alice was a Native American Indian.

would be in fulfilling his farming pursuits. But secretly, she longed for the unique joy of raising a daughter.

Finally on March 22, 1922, their first daughter, Mary Ellen, arrived in answer to Alice's persistent heart-cry. How overjoyed she was to finally have a girl. Two years later God blessed them with another daughter, Betty. Now Alice had two daughters who could eventually help her with the housework.

In 1927 Marvin was born. Allen and Alice were now in high gear, learning how to stay ahead of seven lively children and the ever-increasing demands of the productive family farm.

One day a few years later, Alice was out in the field husking corn. Pregnant again, the drain of physical exertion was rapidly taking its toll. Suddenly, the weariness of work gave way to the overriding contractions of birthing. Well schooled by the many previous pregnancies, Alice immediately headed for the house. Ever sensitive to the needs of her family, she hurriedly set to work baking several extra sweet cakes. Her robust family needed a bit of reserve while she was excused from a few weeks of routine kitchen duty.

Just a few hours later the new arrival was joyously welcomed. There was a strong sense this baby girl should bear the name of her mother, Alice. It was indeed appropriate, since Alice was destined to be her last child. Life was full!

* * *

Mothers are awesome. They spontaneously model a very special brand of practical loving. Godly moms minister this gift in a multitude of inspiring ways. The up-close witness of godly maternal love is one of the greatest blessings children can inherit. Dad was indeed fortunate to have this kind of mother. In addition to her selfless quality, there were numerous other proofs of Mum's down-to-earth godliness showcased daily before her family, all in living color.

Cooking three big meals each day, seven days a week, was in itself no small task. Added to this were the countless other responsibilities necessary to keep the family clean, clothed, and healthy—the home spick and span, functional, and orderly. Mothering and housekeeping in itself represents more work than a typical full-time job. But there was more.

For Mum, farm work was an additional part of her job description. If an extra hand was needed, she could be found milking cows, preparing food items for the milk and produce market routes, or laboring in the fields. She was not only a hard worker herself, but also diligent to instill a disciplined work ethic in her children. Dad definitely received a liberal portion of this virtue from Mum. It's apparent all the brothers and sisters inherited ample doses of the German work ethic—this Clemmerized version.

Mum was a great encourager. Her ministry extended well beyond the bounds of the Clemmer family circle. Motivated as a true lover of people, no sacrifice was too large if it would translate into a blessing for someone else. Her frequent words of comfort and caring were a gift to many. She wrote countless cards and letters, often including a dollar or two to brighten the recipient's day. Mum also used her baking gift to minister encouragement, expressed in the universal language all can understand—food. Her breakfast cakes, homemade bread, and pies were the best! Sick neighbors could always count on a yummy "food visit" from Mum. Well versed in simple home remedies, she was also known to frequently pass along medicinal resources from her own arsenal—goose grease or onion poultices, to name a few.

Mum not only reached out to encourage. She also opened the door of her home, welcoming in a broad cross-section of folks. Alice Clemmer's dining room table provided a natural setting for her gift of hospitality to be expressed. It was common for her to cook Sunday dinners for twenty to thirty guests, served in two seatings.

Several hired men slept and ate under the Clemmer roof for extended periods of time. Dad and his siblings felt free to bring friends home for a meal, to sleep overnight, or to stay for a few days. Guests found the Clemmer homestead to be an inviting, homey gathering place.

In those days, tramps or hobos came by looking for food and a place to sleep. Max, one of these vagabonds who originated from Philadelphia, was a repeat boarder. He came by periodically, peddling dry goods and other wares from his mobile store—a large pack on his back. Max slept on the third floor in the farmhouse attic during his stay at the Clemmer farm. Mum had an endearing way about her, making even these outsiders feel at home.

But beyond all these applaudable attributes, the crowning glory of Mum's virtues was her strong Christian faith. This was not a mere ritualistic form of godliness, confirmed over and over by those who knew her. She loved God and desired to honor Him always. In her darkest hours, Mum seldom complained. Instead, she purposed to identify something to be thankful for. The untimely death of her firstborn, Norman, a young toddler, was an especially painful school for developing this discipline. The dark Depression years of the 1930s also provided another imposed crucible for heartrending faith learning. Evidence indicates she learned her lesson well. Mum's walk with the Lord sustained her through numerous dark nights of the soul.

Routinely, Mum would kneel by the side of her bed for morning and evening prayers. She took seriously the assignment of praying for her family. Other loved ones occupying a place in her heart were included. In addition to these scheduled times of intercession, Mum was also instant in prayer. On one occasion in later years, Dad and his sister, Alice, went to tell their mother about a tragedy in the family. Upon hearing the news, Mum spontaneously got down on her sore, swollen knees and prayed aloud for the situation. Talking with God was a vital expression of her faith.

Dad had an especially close connection with Mum. He learned much sitting at her feet. There is no question—Dad was profoundly impacted by Mum's sincere love for God and the outworking of that love to bless others. The sincere faith of his mother provided a model in the forming of his own faith. This was a valuable legacy, extremely vital in helping Dad tune in to the family destiny.

3

Formative Foundations

Foundations are a vital part of any building. The substance of a foundation usually lies below the ground surface. Though invisible, the composite of mortar and block or stone plays a key role in providing support and strength to the above-ground structure. Foundations in human lives are equally important. They are made up of ordinary elements, in themselves seemingly trivial. Yet, when the unique family surroundings and day-to-day experiences of growing-up years are cemented together, they create a life-shaping foundation to build upon.

I [Jan] love recalling memories of our frequent visits to the farm where Dad was raised. The white-plastered farmhouse was a large stately three-story structure. It had a rambling wooden L-shaped porch. One door led into the kitchen and the other entered directly into the living room. The porch was the perfect place to relax after a hard day's work. Here one could listen to the crickets chirp and savor refreshing breezes bringing relief from the heat of the day.

In Dad's growing-up years, the large kitchen was simple. A well-worn extension table dominated the center of the room. Day after day it was laden with familiar dishes for which Pennsylvania Dutch cooks are famous. Friday was baking day. A large, crude table in the cellar would go from empty in the morning to full by late afternoon. Pies, bread, raised cakes and other mouth-watering baked goods were a main staple in the Clemmer family diet. Each item found its way from basement table to kitchen table in the course of the week.

A cast iron wood range served as the basic appliance for preparing meals. Every morning, someone was assigned the task of firing up the stove. It also served as a primary heat source. Supplemental heat was provided by a space heater, but both sources proved inadequate in making the rest of the house comfortable in winter. This motivated the boys to hustle out for morning chores where body warmth from the cows made the barn a bit more toasty.

The farmhouse had no bathroom, but there was a two-seater outhouse. This was outfitted with corncobs along with catalogs from Sears Roebuck and Montgomery Ward. Since electric lights had not yet been invented, kerosene lanterns were used at night. Electricity finally arrived at the farm in the mid-1920s.

Saturday evening was bath night in preparation for going to church the next day. Mum filled the washtub in the kitchen near the stove and the youngest member of the family used the tub first. On winter Sunday mornings, Mum went to work bundling the children in warm clothes and quilts. Pop hitched up the team of horses and buggy for their three-mile trip to the Franconia Mennonite Meetinghouse. The family bought their first automobile in the late 1920s—a 1925 Hudson. It was a fancy "top-notch" car.

While providing the intimate setting for growing this sizable farming family, the Clemmer homestead acreage was also shared with outsiders. Behind the farmhouse was a medium-sized shed that served as a blacksmith shop. Immediately to the side of the shop was a small overgrown plot of ground where arrowheads had surfaced. Oral family history passed down from earlier generations spoke of an Indian graveyard present there. These below-ground corpses never arose to interfere with the current residents of the farm. Yet, the cemetery served as an ongoing reminder of an "outsider" presence.

Another intruder of sorts leaving a mark on the land was an oil pipeline cutting its path across part of the farm. Later, in the 1940s, a more visible intrusion arrived in the form of electrical high-tension lines with a few huge towers. Though not creating any significant interference, these trespassers served as continual reminders to Dad's family—a very real and diverse world existed beyond the confines of their cloistered family existence.

* * *

Life on the Clemmer homestead was not dull by any means. An enterprising farmer, Pop not only engaged in producing crops, but also marketing them. As with a handful of other dairy farmers, Pop developed a retail route, selling milk house to house for six cents a quart. When the boys came of age, they were given responsibilities to help run the family retail enterprise. In the early days of the business, milk was hand-dipped. Customers set out empty glass bottles on their porch containing money for the next delivery of milk.

Butchering was a weekly happening. Cuts of beef and pork along with related products were marketed to a group of customers in nearby Lansdale. Scrapple was made on Thursday. The meat was cut on the kitchen table and the scrapple mix was stirred in the back shanty. Even the children took their turn at stirring in the mornings before walking to school.

At the age of six, Dad was eager to take his turn in first grade. He had envied his brother, Jake, going off to school with his lunch packed in a lard bucket. The prospect of learning outside the confines of home also held significant appeal. Language was at the top of the list. Dad and his siblings were required to learn English when they started school because Pennsylvania Dutch, a dialect of German, was spoken at home.

The one-mile trek to school took place in all kinds of weather. On cold winter days, the two-room country school was kept warm with a pot-bellied stove. During classes, students eagerly looked forward to sledding during recess. As the days got warmer they enjoyed playing baseball. Girls wore feed sack dresses and boys wore bib overalls and plain shirts. Shoes were worn only in the winter months.

Ida Keyser was Dad's first grade teacher. A small but spirited lady, she was well able to keep wiggly first graders quiet and attentive. Ida's long tenure at Harleysville Elementary extended over several decades. We siblings also had the privilege of getting our start in first grade with

The Allen Clemmer Family. Left to right, front row: Allen (Pop), Alice (Mum). Second row: Mary Ellen, Betty, Alice, Marvin. Third row: Jake, Joe, Bill, Cyrus, circa early 1940s.

Miss Keyser. Occasionally she would remind us about having taught our father. Knowing about this open line of communication between our teacher and Dad helped motivate us to stay in her good graces.

Dad liked school and always hurried to finish daily chores so he wouldn't be late. One morning as Dad was getting ready to go to school, he saw Mum rolling out pie dough. "What are you makin', Mum?" he asked in Pennsylvania Dutch. "Potato pie for dinner," she responded. Immediately Dad negotiated a bargain with Mum. It worked. That day he and his brothers walked home for dinner and then returned to school for their afternoon classes. Potato pie was a worthy reward for the long walk home.

* * *

In the midst of hard work and school demands, humor and fun had a way of spontaneously showing up. As the scriptural proverb indicates, "A merry heart doeth good like a medicine." The Clemmers seemed to enjoy an ample dosage.

One day Dad was working on the tractor in the barn. He was often assigned these repair jobs, having demonstrated a natural ability for fixing things. His sister, Mary Ellen, showed up and became deeply engrossed in watching her older brother at work. Prompted by a spontaneous burst of inspiration, Dad posed his "innocent" proposition. "Mary Ellen, hold the screwdriver for me, will you?" He knew full well the outcome. Since the screwdriver was touching the spark plug, she was set up for a surprising jolt. "Joe!" she screamed. Dropping the screwdriver, she abruptly turned to leave. "I'll get you back!" she threatened, and quickly headed for the house to seek some sympathy from Mum.

A possible inspiration for Dad's love for practical joke-playing was likely supplied by Grandpop Moyer. He was an avid trickster, and the grandchildren fell prey whenever he deemed it appropriate. One beautiful afternoon, Dad decided to take the horse and check on the cows grazing in the back pasture. It was an invigorating ride as the horse trotted through the corner of the woods. Walnut trees interspersed with oaks and maples shaded the path ahead of him.

Suddenly, without warning, he was pelted with a shower of walnuts. Stunned by this unexpected deluge of nuts, Dad glanced at the trees overhead, but saw nothing unusual. Puzzled, he proceeded on his way to check the cows. Everything seemed okay, so he headed back home being careful not to pass under any more walnut trees. A few days later he made a surprising discovery. Grandpop Moyer was the prankster responsible for the walnut assault! Dad had not stopped to consider the possibility of his Grandpop as a fun-loving tree-shaker.

Stan Moyer was one of Dad's favorite cousins. A town boy from Souderton, he frequently visited the Clemmer homestead with the rest of his family. Stan always relished the opportunities for farm fun unavailable in town. He was also especially fond of horses. Soon after arriving one summer afternoon, Dad and Stan headed for the stable. "Hey Joe, how 'bout lettin' me take a ride on Pete," Stan begged, eyeing up Dad's favorite horse.

There in the stall, Pete looked rather docile, but in this case looks were deceiving. Immediately Dad sensed a golden opportunity for some good-natured fun. "Sure, I'll get him out for ya to ride," he responded. Dad always rode Pete without a saddle, so he helped Stan mount, instructing him how to hold on. "Give him a slap on the back after you get started," Dad instructed Stan, with the hint of a scheming grin on his face.

Stan took off, promptly giving the horse his get-up-and-go slap. Pete took off in a mad gallop, catching Stan totally by surprise. Losing his grip on the mane, Stan slid back over the hind end of the animal, and kept on sliding. Frantically grabbing for the tail, he hung on for dear life. In Dad's words, "With eyes as big as saucers, Stan hit the ground running in giant-step strides, too scared to let go!" Suddenly it was all over. Stan was sprawled on the ground as Pete disappeared around the corner of the barn. I'm not sure how much hilarity Dad evidenced in front of Stan, but he sure made up for any lack of laughter when rehearsing the story. It was one of Dad's favorites, and he never tired of retelling about the horse-trick he pulled on Stan.

Dad had lots of humorous growing-up stories that he told and retold, but probably the all-time favorite for us was the one about shooting his brother Jake in the pants. If I recall correctly, it took place during a break after lunch before returning to field work.

"Jake," he called, "go over to the outside cellar door and turn your back toward me. Bend over and I'll shoot at you with the mustard seed gun to see how much you feel it." "Naw," Jake responded, "unless you let me do it to you first." "Sure, no problem," Dad agreed.

Since Dad's pants were baggy even when bending over, it stung a bit, but was tolerable. "Not bad," Dad reported. "Now it's your turn." Jake headed for the cellar door and took his position. "Bend down more," Dad insisted. "I don't want to hit your head!" Jake obeyed, accomplishing what Dad had envisioned all along—tightening the seat of Jake's pants. The instant the shot rang out, Jake exploded in a loud, pain-filled roar. With fire in his eyes, Jake lunged for Dad, and the chase was on. The two headed out the farm lane toward the orchard. Fortunately for Dad, his slender build and long legs kept him ahead of Jake. The chase finally ended when Jake ran out of steam short of making his catch.

Though thankful for his initial escape from Jake's wrath, Dad didn't feel totally victorious. He was well aware of needing to find a way of making up before bedtime. Some sort of a peace pact was a must, since he and Jake had to share the same bed. Apparently Dad was successful. As the story goes, they did end up in the same bed that night, and both lived to tell the story. Oh, by the way, I think Jake's story of that episode was a bit different than Dad's.

* * *

If Dad's shot-in-the-pants story reflects a bit of good natured sibling rivalry, there was also evidence of loyal affection expressed among these eight siblings. One such happening involving Dad that his sister, Alice, vividly remembers took place when she was a five-year-old.

It was a Saturday evening when Mum suddenly realized she had no stockings for Alice to wear to church in the morning. Her old pair was worn out, and too unsightly for Sunday. "Joe, would you run out to the Souder Store and get another pair of stockings for Alice?" Mum asked. "She needs them for tomorrow." Dad agreed to go.

Upon entering the store, Dad headed down the side aisle to where the stockings were displayed. Scanning the selection, he quickly located the style of brown stockings Alice always wore. But close by, he happened to spy a pair of pretty white socks with a small pink flower embroidered on the cuff. Knowing his little sister and her love for pretty things, Dad got a sudden burst of inspiration. At the risk of Mum's disapproval, why not surprise Alice with those pretty socks. She would be thrilled.

He quickly made the purchase and headed home. Mum initially expressed some displeasure, but was able to live with Dad's decision, though it meant overstepping the boundaries of their conservative dress code. The next morning Alice was elated when she walked into church with her fancy new socks. It definitely wasn't the plain Mennonite look!

* * *

These stories are a mere sampling of countless other day-to-day experiences in the Clemmer family history book. Each contributed in some way to shape the foundation of Dad's life. While serving as a primary ingredient, routine everyday happenings were only one ingredient in this foundation-forming mix. In addition to ordinary events, God saw fit to include extraordinary ones as well.

It seems out-of-the-box incidents are especially effective in the formation of spiritual foundations. These episodes typically materialize without warning and have a dramatic or traumatic quality about them. Crisis is one label that seems appropriate for these shaking, making experiences.

Dad encountered his fair share of these. We will look at a few significant ones. These traumatic happenings, coupled with the ordinary ones, established a firm spiritual foundation in the depths of Dad's soul. Yes, significant shaking did occur. But so did the shaping—the breaking and the ultimate making of this man of God.

4

Trauma, Trials and Training

Trials are great training instruments. People used profoundly by God often encounter significant personal crisis along their journey to greatness. Traumatic experiences for a child or young adult can be uniquely formative. Sensitized to the vulnerability and soberness of life at an early age, these persons often become strongly motivated to pursue the Author of Life. This God pursuit "sets them up" to be molded into vessels of honor, fit for the Master's use.

Scripture tells us about Joseph who was sold by his brothers into slavery in Egypt. Later he was mercilessly thrown into prison as a result of a false accusation. David, after being told he was chosen by God to serve as Israel's next king, became the object of a massive manhunt led by King Saul. He lived for years as a hunted fugitive, fearing for his very life. These harrowing life lessons had a way of instilling priceless qualities of humble dependence and progressive faith in David's pliable heart. Each happening prepared him as a God influencer to vitally impact his generation.

Ordinary days repeatedly produce extraordinary sagas. God allowed Dad to be a main character in some unforgettable early-life dramas that shaped his journey in memorable ways. As these events unfolded, Dad had no way of knowing the part each would play in preparing him to fulfill his role as a pioneer leader. Deep in his heart a confidence was being forged. Through each successive experience, there was ever-increasing evidence that God had His hand of favor and destiny upon Dad's life.

One warm summer day, ten-year-old Dad, dressed in a well-worn shirt and denim overalls, went with Jake and his father to work in the hay field. Overgrown fence rows outlined acres of thick grasses ready to be harvested. Scorching rays of the mid-summer sun beat down on Dad's straw hat as he labored with Pop and Jake in the large fields. The strenuous work and intense heat sapped their energy, signaling for a break in the action. But Pop was bent on continuing the aggressive pace. There was hay from one small field to load before they'd quit and head home for supper.

Jake and Dad took their places on the tailgate of the truck, savoring a welcome chance to catch their breath. Pop backed the truck around before heading toward the last field. On an unannounced whim, Jake suddenly jumped off the truck. In a split second, Dad decided to follow. As his feet hit the uneven ground, Dad stumbled, falling directly behind the moving truck and out of Pop's sight. The path of the rear tire was now fatefully aimed at Dad's head. Jake's holler sounded just as the truck wheel crushed the top edge of Dad's straw hat.

Hearing Jake's yell, Pop instinctively jammed on the brakes, bringing the truck to an abrupt halt. With heart thumping wildly, Dad wriggled out from his near-death position, nervously clutching his mangled hat. "Joe, ya okay?" Pop cried in a panic-stricken voice. "Yea, Pop," Dad stammered as a few tears began rippling their way down his grimy cheeks. "It happened so fast. I didn't have time to yell for ya to stop." Dad paused, and then exclaimed with raw emotion, "God saved my life!" No more field work was done that day. With ashen faces and in somber silence, father and sons rode back the rutted field road toward the house for supper.

Glancing up from her steaming kettles on the stove, Mum instantly sensed something was wrong as she scanned the solemn faces of her husband and sons. "What happened?" she exclaimed, seeking a reassuring answer to quiet her intuitive sense of alarm. Pop blurted out the story, with some added bits of detail interjected by both Dad and Jake. Instinctively, Mum went over to where Dad was standing. With tear-filled eyes, she grabbed Dad in her arms, muttering prayer-like exclamations of thanks to God for sparing the life of her son.

Returning to her range, Mum began dishing out evening supper while the remaining family members gathered around the kitchen table. Suppertime was more serious than usual as each family member entered into the emotional soberness triggered by the afternoon ordeal.

That night, as Dad lay in bed, his mind kept mulling over the play-by-play of this traumatic incident. What if that truck wheel had been just a few inches closer to his head? There was no doubt. This earthly life as he knew it would now be history.

Question after question looped round and round in Dad's fatigued mind. One of the reoccurring wonderings was especially haunting—was he ready to die? Suddenly, life felt extremely fragile and fearfully uncertain. Against the backdrop of these haunting questions, a growing conviction began to emerge. Amid this death-laden danger, there was clear evidence the protective shield of the Lord had also been close at hand. As the night wore on, a calming reassurance gradually began sweeping over Dad's anxious soul. His God had definitely been watching out for him. Finally sleep came. Months and seasons passed. Dad had no way of knowing providence was again setting him up for another traumatic experience.

* * *

A prolonged winter had finally given way to the refreshing delight of warm spring breezes. Robins had returned and wild flowers were again making their annual appearance in the surrounding woods and meadows. It was time to spray the apple and peach trees. This job seemed never-ending, repeated seven or eight times each season.

"Joe, don't forget to spray the trees with the wind," Pop reminded Dad as he watched his son methodically testing the sprayer before heading for the orchard. In those days, there was some knowledge concerning the dangers of prolonged exposure to chemicals in poisonous sprays. While attempting to avoid inhaling these fumes as much as possible, many orchard growers failed to use face masks for added protection.

Dad was usually careful to honor safety guidelines while working in hazardous situations. But on this particular occasion, the unpredictable breezes must have caused him to inhale more spray than he realized. Shortly afterward, he became very sick. The doctor was summoned to see what he could do for Dad. "Don't drink any water for thirty days. Just drink ginger ale or porter and stay in bed for a week," Doc Shreiner ordered.

The days passed slowly. Dad didn't relish just laying around, especially in the busy season of spring planting. But he reluctantly abided by the doctor's get-well prescription, gradually reaping the reward of renewed health. There is a good chance those days of being side-lined afforded Dad some time to ponder how God had again watched over him in this newest threat to his physical well-being. With a growing sense of conviction, there could be little doubt that God's merciful and mighty hand was continually covering him with a providential hedge of protection.

* * *

Another ordinary day that turned into an extraordinary trauma experience for Dad was birthed in the chilliness of a mid-December morn. Though an energetic go-getter, Dad reluctantly pulled himself out of bed in order to check his traps. His dog trotted faithfully beside him, a welcome companion on this early morning jaunt.

The first penetrating rays of sunrise were beginning to invade the darkness. Crisp, cold air, though still, caused Dad to hurry his pace. "I wonder if this is a wild goose chase," he muttered under his breath, tramping through the last stretch of stark gray woods on his way to the stream.

Preoccupied in thought, Dad suddenly caught sight of an unfamiliar object in the familiar landscape—a car parked near the edge of the woods. "That's odd," he mused to himself. "Maybe a hunter is waiting until it's time to hunt."

He stood motionless, staring at the car while being alert to any sign of movement within the extended range of his peripheral vision. Out of the blue, it suddenly dawned on him. Hunting season was over a few days ago! There must be some other explanation. Something felt suspicious. Dad decided to quickly check his traps and then return for a closer look at the strange car.

Finding nothing in the traps, he again circled back toward the woods. Dad's heart beat wildly as he cautiously approached the car. Was someone lurking out of sight, poised to attack him? There was something awfully strange and creepy about all this. He kept groping mentally, trying his best to make sense of the situation.

Suddenly, a muted "clunk" from the other side of the car broke the eerie silence. "What was that!" he wondered. Instantaneous fear and panic gripped him. Just then his dog came running around the front side of the car. Immediately Dad interpreted the noise that scared him—the dog jumping on the running board of the mystery vehicle.

Dad inched closer to the car, his eyes fixated to catch any hint of movement. While slowly coming around the rear of the car, he almost stumbled on a dark rumpled object on the ground. With heart pounding uncontrollably, he scanned the sight before him. Dad shuttered involuntarily. There was no doubt. The crumpled form was the lifeless heap of a lady lying on the ground right below the car's rear bumper.

"A dead woman!" he gasped in a startled whisper. Again he studied the ghostly face to be absolutely sure she wasn't breathing. Upon confirming his shocked appraisal, Dad wheeled around and bounded home at top speed with the dog close at his heels.

Bursting into the kitchen where his mother was tending the wood stove he breathlessly cried, "Guess what I found in the woods, Mum. A dead woman!" "Auck, you didn't!" she gasped. "You need to go tell Squire Alderfer. Pop and Jake aren't home, so I'll call over to Sam Erb. He can go with you."

Squire Alderfer listened intently to Dad's story. After some clarifying and questioning, Squire immediately went to work launching an investigation. State officials were notified and they in turn ordered the case to be processed by the Lansdale police.

It wasn't long before the tranquil winter landscape of the Clemmer farm was transformed into a mid-morning beehive of investigative buzz. "Did you touch the car?" the officers quizzed Dad when they arrived at the farm to investigate. "I didn't touch anything," Dad answered with matter-of-fact respect.

On site, the investigation quickly produced some enlightening evidence. Checking inside the car, one officer immediately spied the woman's handbag lying half open on the front seat. "Maybe this will shed some light" he reasoned, beginning a search of its contents. Sure enough, a scrawled note by the woman quickly pieced together her sad story. When an earlier attempt to commit suicide by drinking iodine proved unsuccessful, inhaling fumes from the exhaust pipe was her next death-wish strategy. If that suicide attempt proved vain, a loaded revolver in her purse would be the third and final instrument chosen to seal her personal doom.

After several other incidental questions, the police finally told Dad he was free to go back home. Later in the day, a news reporter arrived to get the scoop from Dad himself. That Wednesday, the Norristown paper carried the complete suicide story, including a picture of Dad standing by the car pointing to the spot where he had found the woman. Through further investigation, it was discovered the mystery woman was a Norristown resident and had worked for the Red Cross. With a documented history of emotional instability, there was good reason to believe the validity of her suicide note.

Years later, whenever Dad rehearsed the story of the dead lady, it seemed apparent he had been deeply moved by that experience. Yet, I don't ever remember him sharing personally out of those depths. Without the benefit of heart dialog, I have no factual commentary on how Dad personally processed being thrust into the middle of this death tragedy. Self-inflicted death was foreign to his sheltered cultural setting. Therefore, this close-up confrontation with suicide must have stirred up some heart-searching questions in Dad's naturally inquisitive mind.

I'm quite certain that for days and months afterward, Dad's thoughts kept reliving his experience of that unforgettable winter morning. Why would someone deliberately kill themselves? What makes a person so depressed they would want to give up on living? God values life and imparts it to us as a present. How does He feel about someone who voluntarily chooses to carelessly squander and destroy their life gift?

Dad probably entertained other questions as he revisited the seriousness of this impressionable occurrence. Having witnessed such an in-your-face example of wasted life, I believe it likely ignited new resolve within Dad, intensifying his passion to fulfill the divine design God purposed for his life. It was a gift too precious to squander. With new resolve, he would live his life to the full.

* * *

It was late morning on a cold day in February. Mum trudged upstairs to spread some wet clothes on a heater in one of the upstairs bedrooms. "This will help them dry quickly," she reasoned as she again hurried down the spiral back staircase to wash dirty breakfast dishes.

Later, having almost forgotten about the clothes, she was suddenly alerted by the whiff of smoke and a faint crackling sound. Even as this warning sounded, the bedroom above the kitchen was being engulfed by smoldering flames. Mum quickly flew into action. Grasping the phone, she began dialing the Harleysville Fire Company just as her mother came running over from the other side of the house. "Go call Pop in from the barn!" Mum hollered.

One mile down the road, six-year-old Alice, seated at her school desk, heard the firehouse whistle sound its alarm. In a few minutes, firetrucks roared past the school. Their blaring sirens indicating the fire to be in the direction of the family farm. Panic and fear gripped Alice's tender heart. A short time later her fears were confirmed as the principal announced the Clemmers were dismissed to be taken home from school. What a shock for all the children as they finally arrived on the scene. Firemen were working feverishly, extending every effort to minimize damages threatening to destroy the entire structure. Alice and her siblings stood there in a daze, viewing the charred remains of both kitchen and bedroom.

Fortunately, a major portion of the house had been salvaged. However, the overpowering smell of smoke permeated every room. It seemed almost impossible for the family to think of occupying their home. Finally Pop and Mum decided that the younger children should be sent elsewhere until the damages to the farmhouse could

An aerial view of the Clemmer homestead, circa 1957. Ownership of the farm had recently been transferred from Marvin to his sister Alice and her husband, Norman Rittenhouse. A large pond was being added (foreground). Behind the house, a large chicken house had recently been constructed, one of the first caged chicken houses in Pennsylvania.

be repaired. The rest of the family would be forced to deal with the inconveniences imposed upon them. They would have to function without their kitchen—the literal hub of family life. In spite of this major inconvenience, life would go on.

A week or two later, in the midst of this misfortune, tragedy dealt its second blow. It was a cold, raw morning. Dad was busily engaged with a wood-working project in the shop. Bill worked with Dad, sawing lengths of wood to be used for their house renovation project. "I'm starved," Bill announced. "I'm gonna see if dinner's ready."

As Bill headed for the house, Dad decided to finish by himself. He was pushing to get the sawing job completed before dinner. Taking the wood in hand, he lined up the plank for his next cut. Though skilled with the circular saw, a knot in the wood caused an unexpected jerk. Dad's hand was suddenly forced into the whirling blade. Instantly, Dad realized he was in big trouble. Even though a spray of blood camouflaged the extent of the wound, it was quite obvious his right hand had taken a big hit. Grasping the wounded hand with his good one, Dad headed for the house. Staggering into the kitchen, pain was now coursing through his entire arm.

The homestead as it appears today. Norman and Alice continue to reside there.

"Joe, what happened?" his mother shrieked as she stared at the gory mess. Little Alice grasped her mother's apron, sobbing uncontrollably as she too gazed at the bloody hand Dad was clutching. Scared, she immediately pictured her dear brother as dying, and couldn't bear to face that possibility. Mum surveyed the seriousness of Dad's injury and yelled for Pop. "You have to take Joe to the doctor right away!" she yelled. Grabbing a clean towel, she frantically began wrapping Dad's hand. Not knowing what to do with the little finger dangling from his right hand, she attempted to keep it properly positioned just as if it were still fully attached. The applied pressure helped slow the bleeding rate. Pop and Dad both ran for the car.

The trip to Doc Shreiner seemed like eternity for Dad, his hand throbbing uncontrollably with excruciating pain. Quickly evaluating the injury, Doc decided to operate immediately. Sadly, the finger could not be reattached. Dad would be uniquely branded and bear that irreversible trade-mark for life—the missing little finger of his right hand.

After surgery, Pop and Mum decided Souderton Mennonite Home would be the ideal place for Dad's initial days of recovery. With their kitchen range still inoperable due to the recent fire, the farmhouse was unusually cold. Uncle Jacob and Aunt Lizzie, Mum's sister, served as superintendents at the Home, and they would give Dad good attention. And so it was that Dad spent a week of his early manhood years at the old folks home in Souderton, living in with a group of aging seniors.

Lizzie and Jacob were a gracious couple, but had no children of their own. In the face of this childless void, they were uniquely motivated to develop personal relationships with their nieces and nephews. This naturally endeared them to the younger generation. Dad really liked Jacob and Lizzie and welcomed this opportunity for extended time with them. Although he enjoyed their pampering, Dad wasn't accustomed to a life of leisure and quickly became bored. Fortunately, he was able to come up with a creative solution.

Life on the farm offered Dad an earned degree in interpreting barnyard sounds. This, coupled with his natural musical ear, made Dad unusually adept at recreating familiar farm animal noises. Always quick to make the best of a situation, he turned to humor as a way of offsetting his monotony. Purposely projecting his voice with life-like realism for the benefit of his around-the-corner audience, he began imitating the "bah" of a sheep. As this life-like animal sound began echoing down the hallway, a white-haired resident next door tuned in to Dad's impersonation. Surprised and tickled, she let loose with an uncontrollable eruption of laughter. The outburst from this oldster was especially noteworthy, since the woman had a reputation for her grumpy, negative disposition. Folks that knew her well declared she had not laughed for years.

Interestingly enough for Dad, his choice to displace self-focused boredom with others-focused entertainment produced a return beyond what he imagined. His off-hand humor had worked a powerful change that even trained doctors and healing remedies were hard-pressed to produce. Humor was a life-changing medicine he could minister—a gift he could easily give.

As recuperation week came to an end, Dad was ready to return home. He welcomed the experiences of normal family living and industrious routines of farm productivity. But it would be several weeks until he could work with his traumatized hand. Even then, the hand would never be "normal" again. Dad would have to live the rest of his life with this loss.

*Dad with one of his first guitars,
on the front porch of the Clemmer homestead, circa early 1930s.*

In evaluating personal limitations, a missing little finger seems proportionately insignificant when compared with many other handicaps people live with. But, for Dad as an instrumental musician, each finger on both hands represented a very precious commodity. Though not as crucial for playing guitar, his right-hand handicap would be much more of a restriction when playing the accordion.

Dad never shared much about coming to grips with this loss. He did end up teaching the accordion, but the keen sense of handicap squelched any motivation to become an accomplished keyboard player. This loss had to have shaped his future musical pursuits, at least to some degree. Without the missing finger, Dad may have developed more interest in mastering the accordion as well as other keyboard instruments. But it seems this limitation actually brought new direction to Dad's musical pursuits, causing him to focus his concentration on playing string instruments. Again, providence was guiding his way.

* * *

There are other significant happenings in Dad's early years, but these recounted ones are especially noteworthy. Each experience contained a precious life-shaping seed that sprouted and matured into a practical understanding of learning to walk with God. These plantings germinated and took root in the rich, dark soil of Dad's yielded heart. In each challenge, God was right there by Dad's side, providing valuable faith-building proof of His practical provision and protection, designed especially for him.

Life is uncertain, but God is sovereign. In event after event, Dad was learning to embrace God and His fathering work—growing to trust the Sovereign One. How masterfully God uses even negative happenings as positive shaping tools to develop character and define calling in His sons and daughters. With each successive incident, Dad was gaining valuable understanding of God, the Potter.

It may well have been these trauma revelations that prompted Dad to eventually choose the song "Have Thine Own Way, Lord" as his all-time favorite. This song became one of the defining ear-marks for Dad's music. Years later, the hymn was to become our opening theme song at each musical program, both the large concerts and other musical events. With every rendering, these words penned by George C. Stebbins became more permanently etched deep within Dad's heart:

> *Have Thine own way, Lord, have Thine own way*
> *Thou art the Potter, I am the clay,*
> *Mold me and make me after Thy will,*
> *While I am waiting, yielded and still.*
>
> *Have Thine own way, Lord, have Thine own way*
> *Hold o'er my being absolute sway*
> *Filled with Thy Spirit till all shall see*
> *Christ only, always, living in me!*

Dad genuinely wanted his heart to be as clay, soft and pliable in the Potter's hand. He had the growing awareness of being uniquely molded by the Master Potter into a vessel to be used in the plan God had for him. With a growing sense of passion, Dad found himself yielding to that process.

Dad didn't know what the future held. But the lessons learned from these unforgettable experiences would be valuable reference points—anchors to hold him steady while encountering overwhelming challenges and trying circumstances yet ahead.

5

Pass It On

The Harleysville Pike was a dirt road back in 1927. Heading from Harleysville to Souderton, you could see the 122-acre Clemmer farm as it lay sprawled out at the far end of a quarter-mile lane. The land deed indicates it was originally purchased from William Penn and passed down from generation to generation since 1718. Initially the farm consisted of 1,200 acres. Through the years, land plots had been sold to various relatives, reducing the acreage. Each year, springtime plowing and planting ushered in the new growing cycle. Warm spring rains would birth new crops of wheat, barley, oats and hay. These same rains also awakened another crop permanently sown in one of the hillside meadows—a stunning perennial carpet of bluebells that bloomed by the thousands. This blue spring flower was destined to make an unexpected but important contribution in the musical destiny of Joe Clemmer.

One day, realizing that his repeated pleas to Pop for a guitar were not about to be honored, Dad decided to solve his dilemma from a different angle. School buddy, Bill Tate, had an old Stella guitar that he would sell for $4.00. The price seemed right. But where in the world could Dad get that much money?

At the time, neighbor Lizzie Heckler would travel each week to Reading Terminal Market in Philadelphia to sell her home-grown produce. City folk flocked to the market, purchasing fresh fruits and vegetables direct from the farm. When spring and summer flowers were in season, Lizzie supplemented her produce sales with fresh-cut floral bunches. For three cents a bunch, Dad picked and picked blue bells and sold them to Lizzie. What a jubilant day when he swapped Bill those four blue-bell-pickin' dollar bills in trade for that guitar-pickin' Stella. At last, Dad had his very own instrument. It seemed too good to be true.

* * *

"Hey, Earl. I'm coming over to visit Jacob and Edna this weekend. I'll bring my guitar along. How 'bout showing me some of what ya know," Dad called as he followed Earl out of the classroom. Earl Alderfer lived in Harleysville right next to Uncle Jacob Clemmer. Dad often met with Earl whenever his parents visited Uncle Jacob and Aunt Edna.

Dad really liked Earl. He was almost like a brother, and downhome fun would often take an adventurous turn. There was that hot summer day when Earl had joined Joe and Jake at the creek. With a careful look to make sure no one was spying, they quickly stripped and jumped into the refreshing waters. Hopefully no one they knew would come by the creek.

There were many other bonding experiences as well, but Earl was special for another reason. He was becoming quite accomplished at picking the guitar. Dad could have looked to other musical influencers. However, Earl was ordained to provide the practical instruction needed in connecting Dad to his musical destiny.

* * *

Work was the password for this era, particularly for these rural German settlers of the picturesque Indian Valley. Even so, a bit of cultural change was in the wind. How noteworthy that formal learning of music was at this time beginning to make its mark in the community.

The Alumni Hall was located on a short dead-end street just off Main in Harleysville. All sorts of community events were held there. Mr. Landenberger, a sought-after music instructor from Quakertown, would travel to Harleysville to conduct group instrumental lessons for interested young people. Children and youth from the immediate locale signed up for instruction with Landenberger. One afternoon after school each week they converged at the Alumni Hall toting an assortment of Spanish guitars, Hawaiian guitars and mandolins. Periodically, Landenberger would combine a few of his musical groups, form an ensemble, and present a recital of string band entertainment for parents and friends.

In addition to Landenberger's teaching program, other unique forms of music-making could be heard coming from the four walls of Alumni Hall. A group of harmonica enthusiasts gathered periodically, combining their musical talents to form a full-fledged harmonica band. All of this was taking place less than two miles from the Clemmer homestead. Though these influences helped provide a musical climate for the Lower Salford Township families, it was Earl and his guitar that most profoundly impacted Dad and helped define the music he was destined to pursue.

Each week, Earl Alderfer made the six-mile trip from Harleysville to downtown Lansdale for guitar lessons. In contrast to the group instruction at Alumni Hall, Moyer Music Studio offered individual string instrument lessons. Mr. Claycomb, an accomplished mandolin player, was one of the primary instructors hired by Moyer to provide private instruction. Earl liked Claycomb and flourished under his tutelage. Earl's dad, Melvin, loved good music and was delighted to see his son picking up the guitar with such enthusiastic diligence.

One day, Earl's dad made a special trip to another music institution in Lansdale—Sloan's Musical Conservatory. Melvin was an excellent singer. His personal interest in vocal music had taken him to the conservatory for vocal lessons under Mrs. Sloan. But on this particular occasion, Mel's pursuit had nothing to do with his own musical interests.

Though not offering guitar instruction, the Sloan's dealings with music wholesalers gave them access to the finest instruments available. The Gibson guitar—Earl had only dreamed of owning such a fine instrument. Of course, his dream was not a secret fantasy. Dads have a way of getting clued in to the longings of their boys. Mel was merely doing what all normal dads enjoy, whenever able. That day, Earl received a significant boost to his budding musical pursuits. Because of a kind-hearted dad who shared his growing passion for music, Earl was suddenly the proud owner of a brand new F-hole Gibson guitar.

As providence would have it, a colorful career was already in the making for this likeable teenage lad. With Gibson in hand, Earl began exploring opportunities to put his talent to work. With high aspirations, his heart was set to perform on the radio. Through a stroke of raw fortune, Earl landed a fifteen-minute radio program on radio station WSAN in Allentown. His dad agreed to sponsor the program with ads promoting the family bologna business. Week after week, this rural farming community joined the broader listening audience, faithfully tuning in to Earl's program. For them, it was a delight to hear their hometown boy pick and sing country favorites made popular by big names like Roy Acuff, Lulu Bell & Scottie, the Delmore Brothers and Jimmy Rogers.

Harleysville furniture store owner, Mandus Bergey, decided to take advantage of Earl's radio success. Contact was made with station WIBG in the flourishing town of Glenside, a suburb of Philadelphia. With Bergey giving financial backing to cover the commercials, Earl was now making an impact to the north and the south of the Harleysville community. Could this be a harbinger of even greater opportunities to come?

Another aspect of Earl's blossoming musical career involved teaching. School buddies and parents had been seeking out this up-and-coming musician for guitar lessons. Dad was certainly fortunate to be among that number. Any observant bystander could see Earl was headed for a multi-colored and successful career in music. But providence has a way of redirecting our lives through unexpected turns. These changes in direction often have a profound impact on the lives of those around us. Little did Earl know how the flourishing family bologna business would alter his anticipated destiny. In the process, it would also profoundly impact the future destiny of his school buddy, Joe.

* * *

"Hey Joe," yelled Earl. "I need to talk to you." Dad's lanky form sauntered down the path from Uncle Jacob's porch and headed for

Sunday afternoon jam session with Dad (on right) and some of his guitar-pickin' buddies. Note two dobro-style guitars (on left) with round metal resonators.

the gap in the hedge. The bushes formed a divider between the two properties. Random thoughts circulated around in Dad's mind as he mounted the steps and greeted Earl.

After a bit of chit-chat, Earl got to the point. "Things are getting hectic with Dad's bologna business. I need to free up some time. Dad wants me to come on board and help him add to our product line and expand distribution." Earl continued to explain his dilemma. Looking intently at Dad he questioned, "Would you . . . will you consider taking some of my students?"

Dad shifted his gaze away from Earl as he pondered the question. Coincidentally, within the past several months, Dad had begun helping a few buddies get started by showing them basic chords. He recalled the satisfaction of helping these guys discover and share his joy of music. But, this proposal was radically different. Did he really know enough to take on an official teaching assignment?

"Earl, I'm not sure what to say. Do you really think I'm qualified to teach?" Dad continued thinking out loud. More questions followed, spontaneously ignited by Earl's unexpected proposal. The two continued to share, deeply engaged in dialog as the shadows lengthened around them.

Later that evening as Dad headed up the road past Sam Erb's house, he wondered what Pop would have to say about this proposal. Accepting Earl's offer would require time away from farm work. Pop never liked it when other activities intruded. He was gaining notoriety in farming circles now extending beyond Montgomery County. Pop was depending more and more upon Dad's skilled involvement and responsible partnership.

Teaching music seemed to be a mighty strange hobby for an ordinary farm boy. And yet, was he an ordinary farm boy? That question had often sought for a satisfying answer in his mind, especially in earlier years. Sometimes Dad half resented his sense of uniqueness. This unsettledness surfaced randomly, but especially when his mother enlisted him for kitchen duty. Helping Mum whip up raised cakes and wash dishes was a bit peculiar for a guy, all right. It felt good to know she appreciated his efforts. Mum worked hard and deserved an extra hand. But he was glad when Betty and Mary Ellen were old enough to be assigned his household tasks.

This reoccurring sense of peculiarity was becoming more intense ever since the "music thing" had gotten a hold of him. Did this teaching opportunity somehow relate? That question was stuck inside his head and would not go away. When would all of this music stuff begin to make sense?

6

The Franconia Frustration

The Franconia Mennonite Meetinghouse is located close to the Route 113 roadway, just a few miles down the road from the Clemmer homestead. Founded in the 1700s, the congregation is housed in one of the oldest and largest Mennonite church structures in Montgomery County. The building's long-standing visual prominence as a stately landmark has parallel spiritual overtones.

Through the years, this congregation has been viewed as an "elder brother" to other Mennonite brotherhoods that were later established. As the number of congregations increased, a conference formed to give oversight on behalf of the denomination. Franconia Conference was the name chosen, apparently due to the prominence of this congregation.

In Dad's growing-up years, church leaders would convene yearly at the Franconia Meetinghouse to conduct conference business. They also addressed spiritual matters of denominational concern. Arriving in their horse and buggies and plain black suits [later with black cars], these bishops and preachers were continually challenged with the task of maintaining the faith of their fathers. Biblical truth needed to be upheld. Rules and regulations promoted a lifestyle and witness of holiness to a worldly society. These righteous standards needed to be enforced. It was important for discipline to be administered by leaders when members of the brotherhood failed to conform.

Franconia Conference identified with the Old Mennonite branch, stemming from their origin in historic Anabaptist roots. Old Mennonites were known at the time as a rather conservative expression of the larger Mennonite faith. New Mennonites were more liberal, and less conspicuous in their lifestyle and dress. Meetinghouses and church life also portrayed other visible distinctions.

* * *

Entering the side door of Dad's church at Franconia, the vestibule led into a large sanctuary area with rows and rows of darkly stained wooden benches. Men sat on one side of the building, and women on the other. Several rows of "amen" benches on either side of the large elevated pulpit area were positioned at a ninety-degree angle, facing the pulpit. Walls were stark and bare, except for several rows of wooden pegs where men hung their large black hats.

In Dad's boyhood days, though English was the primary language used for preaching and singing, Sunday services usually included a representation of German hymns. This was an intentional expression of honoring their Mennonite forefathers and one more way to preserve religious heritage in their rapidly changing world. Sunday after Sunday, Pop gathered up his family. They headed down the long dirt farm lane, out Rt. 113 to the Franconia Meetinghouse. Stepping over the threshold of the side doorway, Dad and Pop entered the distinctive church world of their forefathers. Dad sat in his place alongside his brothers and Pop. At sixteen, he would be allowed to sit with his buddies.

In those days, church leaders usually made their livelihood on the farm. For them, church work was not as much pastoring as it was preaching. Sermons frequently focused on the doctrines of the church, exhorting members to abide by these principles as a basis for pleasing God.

Congregational singing was an important part of each church service. Choristers called out the page number of song selections from the black *Church Hymnal* with red edged pages. The starting pitch for the song was taken from the sounded note of an "A" tuning fork struck on the hard cover of their songbook. Some song leaders who did not read music would depend upon a memorized sense of the song's tonal range without the reference of a tuning fork or pitch pipe.

Month after month, year after year, Dad entered this church world of his ancestors. He participated in the listening, singing, and worshiping, fully immersed in the religious traditions of his fathers. Generations before him had worshipped and expressed their faith in similar fashion. There was no natural reason for Dad to raise issue with the accepted Mennonite way. But somewhere in those mid-teen years, a seed of holy restlessness was born. Something new began to stir within Dad's soul. As he observed the choristers and followed the shaped notes of those familiar four-part harmonies, unexpected thoughts and bothersome questions began to surface.

* * *

It was a warm spring morning. The singing had ended, and Elvin Souder was beginning to preach his sermon. In similar fashion to that of a seasoned lawyer, Reverend Souder went about building his case for living by the laws of God's Word. Though apparently attentive, Dad's mind was secretly embarking on its own journey of deliberation. His growing enjoyment in playing guitar was at the same time introducing a new troubling in his spirit.

Why did his church frown on the use of musical instruments in their worship services? The Bible clearly referenced several instances where harps, cymbals, and lyres were used as an acceptable way to worship the Lord. Though most references about musical instruments for worship occurred in the Old Testament, were there any references given in the New Testament that instruments are forbidden? If playing hymns was permitted at home, why would that same expression not be acceptable at church? There just didn't seem to be any logical answers that made sense. The string of deliberations formed an endless loop, circling round and round in his questioning mind.

Suddenly Dad was jolted back to reality as the congregation arose as one, turning to bow at their bench for Preacher Souder's closing prayer. Dad quickly bowed as well, and then stood with Pop and his brothers for the closing benediction.

As Dad followed Pop out the side door into the bright mid-day sun, he wondered to himself, "Would Pop understand these questions that were haunting him? Did Pop's organ playing ever cause him to consider similar questions about instrumental music and the church?" Pop never talked about it. Had others at Franconia ever felt what he was feeling? If not, why was he different?

7

Straddling the Fence

While finding increased fulfillment in playing guitar, Dad also pursued his escalating love for music within the boundaries of the Mennonite Church. He scrutinized the choristers as they led the congregation in acappella singing.

Song-leading had changed some during the course of Dad's growing-up years. In earlier days, the chorister was not allowed to stand up front to direct the congregation. Instead, he sat on the front bench at the side of the church and led from there. During this era, most of the songs were sung in German. The chorister and the deacon shared in directing the congregation. "Lining" was the term used to describe this team-leading practice. To begin, the deacon would sing a line aloud by himself. The chorister then led the congregation in singing that same phrase. This would continue throughout the entire song.

It was in Dad's early teens that choristers began standing to lead. Having the chorister stand so the congregation could better see his hand motions and hear his voice significantly increased the leader's effectiveness. This change came about largely through the influence of church singing schools. These schools were conducted on Sunday afternoons, attracting significant numbers of teens and young adults. In addition to teaching the rudiments and theory of music, these classes also provided instruction in how to lead congregational singing. Some participated more out of a desire for social interaction than merely to

Dad with his 1930 Chevy, parked in front of the home of his girlfriend, Edith (future wife).

learn about music. But these schools did a great job in training those with a genuine interest in becoming better singers.

Singing schools also introduced young people to the enjoyment of group singing. So it was a natural consequence that out of these training sessions, choral groups began to form. These groups did not perform in church. They sang in homes simply for the enjoyment of making music together. For some reason, male choruses were the most popular.

In his later teens, Dad joined up with Warren Swartley's chorus. Warren was an exceptional vocal musician, with a well-known reputation throughout the Conference. Sitting under Warren's leadership was providential for Dad. Warren, with his contagious enthusiasm, knew how to motivate and energize a group to sing. His passion in leading literally pulled the song out of people's hearts. There is no doubt that Dad received a liberal dose of impartation for energetic song-leading as he drank, week after week, from Warren's well.

Dad not only enjoyed the singing part of his chorus experience, but took advantage of this setting to build new friendships. One that was significant and longstanding was with Wayne Martin.

* * *

Wayne was wired much like Dad. They "harmonized" almost immediately. Not only did these two share a passionate love for music. They also possessed a fervent love for fun. As typical young guys, they'd not likely turn down an opportunity for a bit of "horsing around." The conclusion of chorus practice became an ideal occasion to work in some fun with the guys.

At the time, both Wayne and Dad were driving early 1930s era Chevys. Though Dad never told us about this, Wayne describes one of their favorite antics—"show him the road" racing. In contrast to lining up and drag racing from a dead stop, this racing form took place while driving on one of the country dirt roads. Without any forewarning, the guy following to the rear would suddenly "gun" his car, swinging past the guy in front. This would literally "leave him in the dust," almost forcing the guy to stop and wait for the thick cloud to settle before continuing on.

There were other interesting similarities with Wayne and Dad that kept surfacing in their developing friendship. In the context of church, both Wayne and Dad had a keen love for the scriptures. Because of disciplined self-study, both became gifted Bible teachers.

As Dad was developing his instrumental teaching gift, Wayne began to teach singing. Like Dad, he never had formal college-level training, but developed musical proficiency out of his own disciplined study. Wayne began a singing school in his local congregation at Blooming Glen. A bit later, he moved on to pioneer other schools at smaller mission churches in Perkasie and the rural community of Haycock.

In the midst of all these compatibilities, there was one glaring difference. Wayne was a staunch advocate for acappella music and did not share Dad's appreciation for instrumental music. This difference could have easily jeopardized their valuable friendship. It is quite admirable on the part of both Wayne and Dad how they "agreed to disagree." Throughout their entire relationship, these two maintained a high level of respect and fondness for one another even in the face of this glaring difference.

As seasons of life brought change, the busyness of later years didn't provide time for much interaction between Dad and Wayne. But whenever they had occasion to meet, there was always a warm exchange of dialog. Their conversation reflected the flavor of brotherly love that honors charity over conformity. What a great example of what God intends the witness of his Church to be.

These experiences with Warren Swartley's chorus and the close friendship with Wayne were very special gifts to Dad, especially in the midst of this transitional season. Destined as a pioneer, Dad would eventually move beyond the confining traditional boundaries of Mennonite Church music to fulfill his own musical calling. The lack of understanding and painful criticisms inflicted by the "brotherhood" could have provided sufficient reason for Dad, out of sheer frustration, to initiate a divorce from the church and leave. But he didn't.

Today, as I [Wes] look back upon this chapter of Dad's story, it seems quite evident the "Warren and Wayne" ingredients profoundly protected Dad in this vulnerable time. The hurtful blows from well-meaning protectors of the faith were providentially cushioned by these two men. They provided a valuable lifeflow for Dad within the boundaries of the church.

8

Mom's Roots

God had a unique life and ministry planned for Dad and was preparing just the right partner for him. He would need a gifted spouse to fulfill his God-ordained destiny. It would be important for her to be loving, supportive, and flexible. She would need to be a woman of excellence. In God's providence this woman was born only a few miles from where Dad grew up.

Night was rapidly giving way to early morning light. Martha's sleep had been periodically interrupted as her labor pains became more intense. This was her first pregnancy. The process of labor was a new experience for her. Recalling her mother's description of labor and delivery, Martha felt certain the birthing of her baby was near. Waking her sleeping husband, she asked him to call the doctor. A few hours later on August 9, 1913, God blessed Warren and Martha with a daughter they named Edith.

A few years earlier, Martha Hendricks had married Warren Alderfer in a simple ceremony. Martha's father owned the Hendricks Dairy which was a thriving business in those days. Her husband, Warren, was a hired man on a farm on Ruth Road near Harleysville. This is where they began their married life together. Now their joys were doubled as they welcomed a little daughter into their humble home.

Edith was an easy baby to care for. Her quiet, sunny disposition brought much joy into the lives of this young couple. Martha was

Children of Warren and Martha Alderfer. Left to right: Warren, Martha (twin), Edith, and Mary (twin). The youngest daughter, Erma, is not present.

thankful for the help of her mother as she assumed her own mothering role. Each new thing Edith did was celebrated. It was exciting to watch her grow into a busy toddler.

In the Bible we read the story of Timothy and how he was greatly influenced by his godly mother and grandmother. Edith had four years by herself with her godly parents before other children were born in the home. These were formative years with godly training, preparing her to fulfill God's purpose for her life. Blessed with a sensitive heart, she was being fashioned into a devout woman of God.

One day Warren told Martha about an opportunity to work at the Mainland Creamery. Martha wrestled with the thought of moving. It would be a big task, packing up their growing accumulation of belongings. What would her new living accommodations be like? How would their little girl adjust to the move? On the positive side, she realized this might be a good opportunity for them to advance financially. At the time she had no way of knowing this would be the first of many more moves for their family.

Four years after Edith was born, Martha entered into her second pregnancy. This seemed a bit different than the previous one. She was

Mother with her siblings. Left to right: Mother, Martha, Warren, and Erma, circa 1940s.

concerned about gaining more weight and wondered about the challenges of giving birth to a big baby.

One night Martha unexpectedly awoke with the beginning of birthing pains. As her labor became more intense, she asked Warren to call the doctor. A feeling of relief swept over Martha as the doctor arrived. She was well aware there was little time to spare. "It's a girl," the doctor announced as he delivered their eagerly awaited arrival. While Warren and Martha were gazing at their new daughter the doctor suddenly exclaimed, "There's another baby coming!"

Soon another daughter was delivered into the doctor's strong hands. "Twins. That's why this pregnancy was different than my first one," Martha mused, tears trickling down her cheeks. Filled with wonder and awe, she gazed happily at her two new daughters. What should they name these girls? How would she care for twins? Her days and nights would be extremely busy. On and on Martha's thoughts rambled as her weary body finally relaxed into an exhausted sleep.

Edith adjusted well to Mary and Martha's arrival, making room for their noisy invasion into her tranquil world. She rallied to the call of duty and became a big helper to her mother. Grandmother Hendricks, just a few doors away, was close at hand and also welcomed the opportunity to help care for these newborns.

Sixteen months after the birth of the twins, Martha gave birth to a boy who was given his father's name, Warren. Another daughter, Erma, was added to complete the family circle. Martha's life was now consumed with caring for her rapidly growing family. Her in-charge manner and strong faith in God were assets during these demanding days and nights.

* * *

Edith began first grade at the Mainland School. A diligent, conscientious student, she kept busy with her school work and faithfully performed household chores. When the family relocated, the children transferred to the Fry School. The building still exists along Kriebel Road, now serving as a family dwelling. This was a one-room school with grades one to eight. Students sat at double desks, each one capable of accommodating two students. Sometimes when the teacher was busy, older students were enlisted to help younger ones with their studies. They took turns going outside to "clap" erasers, and were expected to help the teacher in other ways as well.

Edith especially enjoyed art, reading, and penmanship. Large maps were pulled down over blackboards for studying geography. Reverend Brendle and his wife taught during that era. Endowed with a personal love for music, they emphasized this subject with their students. At recess the children played baseball, tag, hide and seek, and blind man's bluff.

Sometime later Edith's dad took a job in a creamery near Unionville. This move took her to the Fairhill School. A few years later, she transferred to the Airy Hall School on Troxel Road. After graduating from the eighth grade, Edith secured a job at Dexdale Hosiery. She was employed as a factory worker for seven years.

Numerous geographical moves and school changes were a unique training ground for Edith. God was forging qualities in her that would be needed in the unconventional life he had designed for her. The final move took the Alderfer family to a farm near Lansdale. Edith's parents spent the rest of their lives on this attractive farm along Troxel Road.

Edith's grandparents lived on the other side of the house. They had great respect for Martha, the wife of their son, Warren. They affirmed the way she handled her children, often commenting how quiet she kept the family of four children next door. Martha was described as a good mother who had things under control without raising her voice. She was also a submissive, encouraging wife to her quiet hard-working husband.

As the oldest child, Edith was a great help to her mother. When she was growing up, Edith was frequently described as a "little mother." She seldom complained when needing to tend her younger siblings, and seemed to have a double dose of patience. That quality kept developing even more fully throughout her adult years. Edith accepted the Lord as her personal Savior as a teen and was baptized on Dec. 20, 1931. As a young lady, she was serious about her faith. Though quiet by nature, her witness was unmistakably evident to her family and friends.

It was only a few years later that Edith's dad began suffering from

Warren Kratz Alderfer (1892-1938) father of our mother, Edith, with his horse and carriage on Main Street, Harleysville, circa 1910.

heart-related difficulties. Fortunately, neighbor and friend, Doc Jacobs, was close at hand and attended to Warren. But after a four-year battle, the illness finally took its toll. On December 7, 1938, Warren died at age forty-six. This happened to be the birthday of his son, Warren. While visiting at the home of his girlfriend and future wife, Naomi, Warren received the phone call with the shocking news about his dad.

Processing the loss of husband and father was very difficult for the family. Even though they were thankful his struggle with pain and suffering had ended, his absence would be keenly felt. Their lives would never be the same.

Warren's favorite song, "Safe in the Arms of Jesus" was sung at his funeral. This song provided special inspiration to the family in the days and years that followed. No wonder it became one of Edith's favorites. Martha was left to cope with life as a young widow. Many times she grieved silently and wept alone in the wee hours of the morning. How could she go on another day without her husband? At this time she had no way of knowing how the Lord would faithfully sustain her through thirty-one years of widowhood.

It was Martha's disciplined walk with the Lord that carried her through the various trials of life. She experienced God's comfort and then passed on comfort to hurting people around her. Sensitized through her own loss, the Lord used Martha's empathetic personality to bless the lives of other women in their times of crisis.

Girls are blessed when they have godly mothers. Edith was blessed with a god-fearing mother who demonstrated the sterling qualities of a meek and gracious spirit. She witnessed Christian love in action lived out in the home. The mothering example of Martha coupled with her desire to please God instilled Christ-like characteristics in Edith that were effectively modeled for us.

God certainly was preparing a wonderful helper for Dad. Together they would become a dynamic team in fulfilling the wonderful plan God had for their lives.

9

Edie My Sweetie

Just a few traces of summer evening sunlight lingered on the western horizon as Dad and one of his buddies drove down the backcountry road. Each fellow had a girl by his side. According to Dad's version of the story, at one point, he pulled out his guitar and began playing and singing one of his favorite songs.

> *Down in the valley, valley so low*
> *Hang your head over, hear the wind blow*
> *Roses love sunshine, violets love dew*
> *Angels in heaven know I love you*

Occasionally Dad stole a glance at the lovely girl by his side, hoping for a positive reaction. Earlier that evening, Dad and Raymond had gone to the young people's meeting at Plains Mennonite Church. Local Mennonite congregations took turns having Sunday evening services for the larger church community. This was a convenient way for teens to get acquainted with peers from other congregations. As dating-age guys sat with the older men on one side of the church, their wandering eyes glanced across the aisle to the pretty young ladies on the opposite side.

On this particular evening, one girl seemed to stand out to Dad. He recalled seeing her there at a previous service. But this night, something felt different. After the service ended, Dad stayed to chat with a few of his buddies. Though engaged in conversation, he kept a watchful eye, making sure she wouldn't leave without him knowing. There was something about Edith Alderfer that made his heart stir.

Finally she and one of her friends left the church grounds. They started walking out Troxel Road, leisurely strolling toward the Alderfer farm. Dad and Raymond jumped in Raymond's Chevy and took off. Pulling up alongside the girls, they presented their offer for a ride. Dad motioned for Edith to sit in the back seat with him. Katie climbed in the front with Raymond.

The couples enjoyed some light-spirited conversation, and Dad also invented a way to mix in a bit of music. Yes, for some reason the guitar was also accompanying him that evening. Then all too soon it was time to take the girls home. Dad knew he wanted to spend more time with Edith. It wasn't hard to know why he was attracted to her. Edith seemed to have a way about her that was charming and unusual. She certainly wasn't the "giddy" type like many of the girls her age.

Edith had a difficult time falling asleep that night. Not only was Dad tall, dark, and handsome but he was easy to talk to and had a contagious sense of humor. She was also impressed by his music-making abilities. There were numerous things about Joe Clemmer that intrigued her. He seemed different than other fellows she knew. It was exciting that he had asked to see her again.

After this eventful evening they only dated occasionally since Dad's mom didn't want him to go steady until he was eighteen. Each time together was special as their romance blossomed and matured over the months. Sunday afternoons were spent riding around to attractive outdoor spots in the area. For evening dates, they frequently attended church meetings. Afterward it was customary to play games at the home of friends.

Edith was well liked by Dad's family. Her quiet, friendly personality quickly won the approval of the entire Clemmer clan. The Alderfers approved of Dad from the very beginning. His humorous outgoing personality awakened a fresh breath of joyfulness in their home. They liked hearing him sing and play as they were going to bed at night.

One hot summer day Dad was mowing the yard at Edith's place. She had heard that one of the ways to a man's heart is through his stomach.

As the oldest child, Edith had a good amount of experience cooking and baking. Early in their relationship, she discovered Dad had a "sweet tooth" and was especially fond of pies and cookies. While he was busy mowing, Edith went to work making him a Quakertown Crumb Pie. Fortunately, it came out of the oven a true winner. As Dad's taste buds came in contact with the delicious molasses goo, crumbs, and flaky crust, he was instantly awestruck with Edith's outstanding culinary skills. This along with her sweet, tender personality really wowed him. What a gal! This may have been when he began calling her "Edie, my sweetie!"

After a four-year courtship, Dad asked Edith to marry him. His love had captured her heart and she had already decided Joe Clemmer was the man for her. Without hesitation she agreed to become his wife. They marveled at God's goodness in bringing them together. Now they could put plans to their dreams with the priority of establishing a godly home.

Early the next morning after Dad's proposal, he entered the milk house. His mother was already busy, washing the glass milk bottles. Mum enjoyed working with Dad. She treasured the meaningful talks and spontaneous humor they experienced together. Through the years Dad had been an obedient, responsible child. He had matured into a fine young man. As she looked up, she noticed a twinkle in her son's eyes. "He seems especially light-hearted and energetic this morning," she thought to herself.

"Mum, last night I asked Edith to marry me, and she said yes," Dad exclaimed. "Oh, Joe, I'm so happy! She will make a wonderful wife for you," Mum responded warmly. Her eyes swelled with tears of joy as she gave her son an intimate hug. Going back to her bottle-washing work, Mum's heart soared as she pondered this exciting news.

Dad and Edith's one year engagement was busy as they planned for their wedding. Edith prepared household items for her hope chest. Dad worked diligently saving money to care for his future wife. Life took on a brightness and sense of anticipation he had never imagined.

* * *

June 20, 1936, dawned bright and clear. The sun was beginning to showcase its awakening glow across the eastern horizon as Dad drove

Pop's huckster truck through Harleysville on his way to Lansdale. This was his usual Saturday morning market run, but today was no ordinary day. It was his wedding day! However, there was lots of work to do before that glorious event. Dad plunged into the day's activities with an external zeal that mirrored the internal excitement of his heart.

Dad enjoyed selling produce. He was a natural-born salesman. Customers responded to his charisma and warm, engaging personality. Dad always expressed interest in their world, and had a unique ability to bring a fresh burst of sunshine into their lives.

The topic of conversation this particular Saturday was a bit different—his marriage to his darling, Edie. As Dad enthusiastically told his customers this was his wedding day, they shook their heads in disbelief. "You're getting married today!" they exclaimed. "Why are you out here working?" If they had really known Dad, these customers would not have been that shocked. It certainly wasn't contrary to the nature of Joe Clemmer to work hard on his wedding day.

The busyness of serving customers helped the hours to fly by. Finally Dad was headed home to accomplish his real mission of the day. As he sped in the long farm lane, Dad glanced at his watch. The Elgin registered four o'clock. With their wedding scheduled to begin in an hour, this was pushing it close.

Dad hurriedly donned his new fifteen dollar suit and the shoes he had bought for three dollars. Getting ready in record time, he quickly drove to Edith's place to pick up his bride. Arriving at the front door, Dad's heart skipped a beat when he saw how gorgeous Edith looked in her light blue wedding dress. Could it really be true that Edith Alderfer was soon to be his wife? The tantalizing aroma of delicious food wafted through the breeze as Dad and his future bride pulled away from the Alderfer farm. Edith's family was busy preparing a wedding feast for the family and friends invited to share in celebrating this memorable event.

Two minutes before the wedding was to begin, they arrived at the preacher's house. Their attendants, Jake Bechtel and Verna Kulp, had already arrived. They were nervously eyeing the clock. Everyone took their place and the service began. J.C. Clemens, Edith's neighbor and minister, led them through the traditional wedding vows. After the "I Do" exchange between bride and groom, the service was concluded.

Following a celebrative ride in the local area, they returned to the Alderfer farm. Twenty-five guests had gathered to celebrate this special occasion with them. The delicious meal and wonderful fellowship added a festive note to their wedding. This would be a treasured day to remember and celebrate through the years!

The next day, Sunday, the Clemmer farm was buzzing with activity. Dad's mom was preparing a sumptuous meal for forty-five guests. She was pulling out all the stops, intent on making this a fitting celebration. Other members of the household were also engaged in the preparation process. Excitement saturated the air. Mum was busy thinking as she worked. Oh how she would miss her son, Joe. He had been such a dependable worker. The demands of the hour prevented her from dwelling too long on this vivid sense of loss. Quickly wiping her hands on her feed-sack apron, Mum reached into her china closet to get another serving dish.

Just as she was putting her finishing touches on the meal, the last guests arrived. Everyone sat down to the bountifully laden tables and became quiet. Pop thanked God for the newly married couple. He also mentioned the blessings of family, good health, abundant food, and wonderful friends. The kitchen and dining room resonated with lively conversation and bursts of humor as Dad and Mom celebrated with their family and friends. As after-dinner chatter subsided, the younger men went outside to play croquet while the women washed and dried dishes. One by one, families said their good-bys and headed home to conclude this red-letter day.

Dad and Mom didn't go on a honeymoon vacation. However, three days after the wedding, they took a trip to New York City to pick up some musical instruments. Mixing pleasure with business, Dad and Mom toured the Empire State Building, visited a few other sights in the city, and finally headed for home.

In those days, a trip to New York was quite an excursion. Pulling up to the Clemmer farmhouse later that evening, Mum welcomed them with a rather amusing greeting. "Joe, you couldn't find New York, could you. That's why you've come back so soon!" Never having traveled outside the state of Pennsylvania, New York seemed to Mum like a far and distant land—virtually inaccessible. Dad smiled broadly,

Dad and Mom's formal wedding photo, June 20, 1936.

assuring her their trip had gone as planned. He had found New York City and had the instruments to prove it.

* * *

For these two, married life got its start on the Alderfer farm. With a desire for a home of their own, they kept their eyes open for just the right place. Two years later, Dad spied a sale bill listing some property to be auctioned off along Route 113. He was immediately interested since the land was located only a quarter mile from the Clemmer homestead.

On the sale day, Dad took Pop along with him. Standing on the edge of a small crowd of onlookers and bidders, Dad wasted no time getting in on the action. After a few bids, the asking price for the 200' x 200' building lot had risen to one hundred ninety dollars. It was Dad's turn to bid, and he took a few moments to confer with Pop. Under his breath, Pop muttered, "That's too much money. Land prices will come down, but you do what you want."

It seems Dad's pioneering spirit kicked in—he decided against Pop's advice. The location was perfect, even if the price was a bit high. Signaling the auctioneer, Dad took the risk and placed what became the deciding bid. The one-acre property was his, all for two hundred dollars. Time has proven that Dad's purchase was a whale of a deal. He never regretted that investment.

Building a new home was a daring venture for a young couple in the late 1930s. Contractors Swartley and Clemmer were hired to build the sizable two-story, three-bedroom red brick house with dormers. Construction began in March and was finished in August. The house plus a two-car garage cost eight thousand five hundred dollars. After moving day, a number of friends came to visit. They were eager to look over the appealing features of this attractive house.

Dad delighted in the opportunity to make their new house a home. He took pride in providing a comfortable place for raising a family. The fulfillment of his dreams with "Edie my Sweetie" were just beginning.

The house Dad and Mom had built along Route 113 between Harleysville and Souderton, circa early 1940s.

10

Sound of the Islands

It seemed like just a normal day. Dad was in the huckster truck headed down the Sumneytown Pike toward Lansdale. The truck labored a bit, loaded down with an abundance of fresh farm produce. Getting into the homes of these townsfolk of different ethnic backgrounds was a welcome change from the mundane routine of farm chores. Dad grabbed the market basket and briskly headed down the street. There seemed to be a hint of rain in the air, so he needed to keep moving.

As Dad mounted the front porch of his first customer and reached to give the door a firm rap, he suddenly stopped short. What was that sound? He listened. The opened window of the adjoining house framed the appealing sounds of guitar music. But the sound was distinctly different than what Dad played. He listened intently. No, it was not radio music. The sliding tones were intriguing.

Someone was practicing Hawaiian guitar. Though he had heard "slide guitar" played on some of Roy Acuff's records, this style of picking seemed more like the true Hawaiian sound. He just stood and listened.

Suddenly, the door of his customer opened and the lady exclaimed, "Joe, I didn't even hear you knock." Dad grinned impulsively and immediately launched into his familiar sales pitch. "Our sweet corn is the best yet this season—just picked this morning and as sweet as sugar." He quickly made the sale and turned to leave. As the door closed behind him, Dad's long legs hurried down the walkway, carrying him quickly toward the sound of that guitar.

Now at the door, Dad's knock brought an abrupt halt to the guitar music. Almost instantly he was facing the maker of that silk-like sound. The fellow glanced at Dad's market basket. "I was next door and couldn't help hearing your guitar," Dad stammered, searching for the right words. "How about playing some more." He paused, and then continued on. "I play Spanish guitar but would really like to learn the Hawaiian as well. Do you take lessons? What kind of music do you use?" Dad was struggling to stay calm, but inside he was about to burst.

Several minutes later Dad was hustling down the sidewalk toward the truck. The first sprinkles of rain were beginning to fall. He'd have to try and make up this lost time somehow. Dad kept repeating the name over and over under his breath. Eddie Alkire. He checked his pocket once more to make sure not to lose the little piece of paper with Eddie's name and address scrawled on it.

Dad had never been to Easton, but he sure was going to find a way to get to meet this Alkire musician. Wow, that would be quite something to meet a true-to-life music composer. He just had to find a way to get some of that music. This was certainly an answer to his unspoken heart-cry. And to think he had found out about Eddie and his Hawaiian music while working his market run. Amazing!

As the huckster truck retraced its route that afternoon and turned into the farm lane, Dad thought to himself, "Had I been tied down to the farm, I would never have heard about Eddie." Little did Dad know how significantly this new piece would fit in with his music-making future.

Later that week, a letter passed through the hands of the Harleysville postmaster mailed from this aspiring novice to the professional guitarist in Easton. Several days later, a packet arrived with several pieces of sheet music and a personal note from Eddie. This was the spark needed to ignite fresh passion within Dad to expand his musical pursuits. Somewhere, Dad got a guitar that he adapted with a conversion nut for Hawaiian-style playing. Instantly, the spark was transformed into a blazing flame—a flame destined never to be extinguished.

Eddie's instruction course included some traditional songs, but majored in Hawaiian pieces such as "Aloha Oe", "Hilo Pride of Hawaii", and "My Isle of Golden Dreams". Dad worked diligently to master these tunes. There was something so fascinating about the slide of those notes connected together by the glide of his bar. No sound on the face of this earth compared with it.

As the months marched on, Dad's playing ability continued to improve. It was enjoyable picking these standard Hawaiian tunes, but this music was not his first love. What would it be like to use the unique sounds of the Hawaiian guitar to play God-honoring songs of the church? Now that was a wild thought!

* * *

Eddie Alkire was the first professional musician that Dad was exposed to personally. Eddie, like Dad, had very humble beginnings. His history began in the remote mountain heartlands of Hacker Valley, West Virginia. Eddie's deep love for music and the lure of the uncommon drew him, like a magnet to this fascinating instrument—the Hawaiian steel guitar.

As a young budding musician in his early twenties, Eddie left his coal company employment as an electrical engineer to work for Oahu Music Company. Oahu was birthed in Cleveland, Ohio, as a music studio and publisher. Capitalizing on the Hawaiian guitar craze of the late 1920s, they later branched out to manufacture guitars.

Already demonstrating unusual musical aptitude as a composer, Eddie was hired to write music for their publishing division. This job fit well, allowing him to continue pursuing his career as a musician. Shortly afterward, Eddie landed a position with the Oahu Seranaders, a major network group. These entertainers performed on over 1000 coast-to-coast broadcasts for NBC and CBS during the first years of network radio. Along the way, Eddie also secured solo recording contracts with big name labels like Decca and Columbia Records. This popularity as a steel guitarist became quite satisfying for Eddie. Yet, the deeper motivation of his heart was to be fulfilled as an educator and innovator.

After moving to Easton, Pennsylvania, Eddie went to work publishing and marketing his own Hawaiian guitar instruction course.

This curriculum blended the basics of traditional music notation with Eddie's system of creating symbols to identify specific patterns of picking. The course included well over 100 songs. What he created was a truly remarkable feat. Due to Eddie's national notoriety as an entertainer, aspiring guitar players across the country were made aware of Eddie's guitar method. They purchased the sheet music course through his mail-order company.

Though Dad was able to get started with the first packet of music from Eddie, he knew the only way to make real progress in his playing was to take lessons. Easton was a fair distance away, but traveling those miles would be worth it to have Eddie as his instructor. Dad's pioneering perseverance kicked in. Taking action, it landed him a spot on Eddie's roster of students.

Eddie assumed a typical teacher's posture with Dad. But it wasn't long until these two began to connect as friends. Their common love for humor became a great bonding agent. They naturally played off one another with a spontaneous, witty flow. After several months, Dad invited Eddie and his wife, Majorie, to spend a social evening with Mom and him at their home in Harleysville. This relational connection was a providential setup. Eddie and his pioneering gift would prove to be one of the most significant ingredients in helping Dad fulfill his own destiny as a pioneer musician.

* * *

True pioneers are never satisfied. They cannot sit still. Their minds are continuously in gear, envisioning new and better ways to create, build, and advance. When others see problems, they see potential. When facing obstacles, pioneers climb over them in faith and keep on going. They prepare the way for others to follow.

While enjoying his success as an innovative music educator, Eddie was also exploring an ingenious pioneering dream—creating a new breed of Hawaiian guitar. Traditionally, the Hawaiian was constructed as a six-string guitar, tuned to an open chord. A bit of experimentation with other tuning variations was being done by a few guitarists. These alternate tunings opened new possibilities to adapt the Hawaiian guitar for playing other styles of music. Eddie tinkered with some of these new tunings, but was not satisfied with the results.

A crucial problem remained unaddressed, even with these tuning variations. Each was still based on a specific chord, presenting significant limitations when playing in other keys. To overcome this challenge, some guitar makers and performers were custom designing their guitars with more than one neck. These double and triple neck instruments did improve playing versatility. But they were too large to be played like the traditional lap steel. Instead, they had to be mounted with screw-in telescoping legs. These bulky instruments were extremely cumbersome for traveling entertainers.

Eddie's creativity led him to pursue another direction of exploration—designing a lap guitar with a few extra strings and a totally different tuning approach. Rather than tuning the strings to a specific chord, Eddie devised a tuning with smaller intervals similar to successive notes on the piano. The end result was a ten-string Hawaiian guitar which he named the EHarp (pronounced "ay-harp").

The two innovations—adding four extra strings along with using a chromatic-based tuning automatically opened up endless new possibilities of playing. With the EHarp, Hawaiian instrumentation could now easily cross over into other musical styles, even the complex world of classical music.

Eddie secured the assistance of Epiphone Guitar Co., a top-quality guitar manufacturer, to build the EHarp. Introduced in 1940 at the 38th Annual Convention of the Guild of Banjoists, Mandolinists, and Guitarists, this exposure transformed Eddie's dream into a music pioneering reality. Though having enjoyed significant notoriety from his success as a musician, Eddie's EHarp launched him to even greater heights of recognition. Prestigious groups like the American Guild of Musicians placed him in the elite company of world renowned musicians like Tommy Dorsey and Fred Waring. For Eddie, this meant receiving recognition and awards reserved for the great musicians of his generation.

* * *

Eddie was intrigued with Dad's love for sacred music. Though not having a natural inclination toward this style of music, Eddie's developing friendship brought him into close proximity to the musical stirrings of Dad's heart. These two musicians, very diverse in their personal and musical history, shared an uncommon unity on two essential fronts—a passionate love for the Hawaiian guitar and the creative motivation of a pioneer.

An unusual partnership was birthed out of this "heart and calling" connection. It was definitely a case of "deep calling unto deep." A providential dynamic was at work. This grace enabled them to overcome what could have been formidable obstacles. Dad was not intimidated by Eddie's genius-level musicianship. Eddie did not feel out of place relating with Dad, nor was he reluctant to accept Dad's invitation to explore the "foreign" world of sacred music.

Some of those memorable "jam sessions" took place in our living room. I [Wes] can still picture these two musicians, side by side, fully engrossed in their guitars and their music. Though it seemed a rather ordinary happening at the time, those sessions now seem profound. This was especially so when Eddie was creating colorful Hawaiian arrangements for the slower, meditative hymns like "Sweet Hour of Prayer", "Cleanse Me", and "Near to the Heart of God". Without defacing the simplicity of the inspirational melody lines, Eddie's intricate harmonies transposed these old compositions into "new songs" of praise to God. I wish I could know what Dad felt at those moments. Favorite songs of his heart were being recreated and imparted to him through the mastery of his genius friend, Eddie. They must have been soul-stirring. What an awesome gift of inspiration to fuel Dad's flame!

Dad with his EHarp, a ten-string Hawaiian guitar invented by Eddie Alkire, Easton, Pa.

11

Family Callings

In scanning the picture of what was unfolding through Dad's "out of the box" musical pursuits, it seems apparent—Dad was being propelled by his calling as a pioneer.

Pioneers are trailblazers. Trailblazers are motivated to create a path where there is none. These risk-taking individuals are willing to sacrifice so others who follow can enjoy a better future. Forerunners see and pursue that which is not yet understood and accepted by the majority. Therefore, pioneers are often criticized and opposed.

Dad had his share of critics. As is often the case, much of the razzing and digs he received were subtle. These remarks were frequently couched in humor and spoken by those who appeared to be friends. I [Wes] can recall overhearing the joking observation, "Joe plays for a living." These jabs were made by peers in the midst of social conversations. Bystanders would inevitably respond with a good-natured laugh, but imbedded in some of those chuckles was a touch of mockery.

Dad's musical pursuits did not fit the Mennonite mold. Most of his church cronies were traditional thinkers, and extended very little grace to those of their own who strayed "outside the box." Ironically, while opposing Pioneer Joe Clemmer, these critics were at the same time applauding Pioneer Allen Clemmer. Blinded by inflexible short-sightedness, they failed to see and affirm the significance and blessing of family callings at work. Pop's similar trailblazing nature, though not expressed through music, was expressed in his pioneering approach to farming. For this Allen Clemmer was well known.

The Moyer homestead was among the largest farms in the area. Pop had acquired it from his father-in-law, William Moyer. It was a great piece of land. Immediately, Pop began making his own significant mark in the local agricultural community. As an avid reader, he would make frequent trips to the local library. Pop aggressively searched out books and periodicals that addressed innovative trends in farming. He was a risk-taker, ready to try his hand at new and promising agricultural ventures.

Allen Clemmer was among the first in Lower Salford Township to plant and cultivate a large acreage of fruit orchards. Fruit-growing represented a lot of hard work. Pop and the boys planted the trees, did the spring pruning and sprayed the entire orchard several times each season. At harvest time, they would pick fruit most of the day, and after supper, grade apples till 9:00 at night. This was definitely not for the faint-hearted.

At another time, he got wind that farmers in Maine were making good money raising potatoes. After doing his research, the family work-crew planted potatoes, and potatoes and potatoes. A year or two later, wanting to increase his yields, Pop traveled with a farm tour to Maine and Prince Edward Island. He hoped to discover, first hand, the secret to their great success. The trip in itself was quite a bold venture in those days, but no big deal for a true pioneer.

Similar stories could be told of his other trailblazing pursuits— bottling and delivering milk from his own dairy, raising sheep and beef cattle. Whatever trend was being heralded as the farm opportunity of the future, Pop would immediately jump at the chance to "pioneer" it in his locale. As a boy growing up, Dad flourished in this innovative environment. His pioneering spirit resonated with his father's.

In Dad's boyhood years on the farm, Pop certainly recognized his son's instinctive ability to fix things and to come up with innovative solutions for repairing broken-down farm equipment. Dad was always improvising and making use of what was at hand. No doubt Pop delighted in Dad's ingenious abilities. He probably embraced a secret hope that the pace-setting reputation of the Clemmer farm would continue under Dad's able leadership.

The decision to choose music over farming had been a very difficult one for Dad. He did not make that career choice on a whim. Dad loved farming. It was a vital and fulfilling part of his life. He found enjoyment in working the soil, tending the animals, operating the equipment, making repairs and initiating creative renovations around the farm. He was accustomed to working hard. The mix of farming during the day and teaching music students in the evening was initially no problem. But as the demand for lessons continued to multiply, something had to change.

It finally came to the point where Dad knew he had to make the choice. Having a sincere sense of wanting to follow God's lead, he prayed for clear direction. Over and over he questioned the Lord, "What am I called to—music or farming?" Dad agonized over the decision. And he continued praying. Sensing this choice represented a vital turning point in his life, Dad didn't want to make a mistake.

I [Wes] can remember him retelling this "crossroads" story many times. Usually it was shared with visible emotion. He would conclude by saying, "Immediately after I asked the Lord to show me which way to go, several calls came in from parents wanting music lessons for their children. I took that as a sign from the Lord saying I was to lay down farming and pursue music."

On the surface, Pop did not strongly resist Dad's descison to leave the farm and choose teaching music to earn his living. Marvin was ready to step up and take the farm which made it less painful to release Dad. But underneath there was probably sadness that Dad had not chosen to follow in his footsteps.

In those days, the ultimate dream and fulfillment for most fathers was to have a son choose the same occupation that he himself enjoyed. This often included the satisfaction of passing on family farms and businesses from generation to generation. Parents recognized and affirmed offspring who followed in their footsteps and did what they could to promote it. But this sense of family connection and calling was typically understood in terms of externals—careers, talents, personalities and natural resources. Relatively few had the awareness of God imparting specific callings and purposes upon family lines—unique family potential to be passed on from generation to generation.

* * *

A front porch teaching session. Dad is far right with Warren, brother of Edith, next to him, circa late 1930s.

One of the most inspiring biblical examples of family callings is the father-and-son story of David and Solomon. David's lineage, traced back over preceding generations, was rooted in the tribal family of Judah. There was a clearly defined sense of leadership calling written into the DNA of Judah's family line. In the Genesis 49 account, a calling of leadership is prophetically spoken over Judah by his father, Jacob. "The scepter shall not depart from Judah, nor the ruler's staff from between his feet . . . "

This family calling upon the line of Judah surfaces over and over again in sons and generations that follow. Centuries later, David aggressively identifies with this visionary leadership calling in multiple ways, but none more profound than as a conquering warrior. His heart to see the people of God in full possession of the promised-land inheritance inspired him to lead the charge. It was under the God-favored military leadership of David that Israel was enabled to conquer the land of promise and establish its kingdom.

Because of his intimate friendship with God, David didn't merely view this military quest as an end in itself. He somehow had mined the deep recesses of God's heart and thereby discovered the Lord's ultimate intention for the nation of Israel. It was about more than the people and the land. God also wanted to dwell there right in the midst of these chosen people bearing His name. In other words, Father wanted to be close to His children.

The wheels of David's visionary leader mind continued to turn. For God to reside in the land, He needed a house. So David automatically assigned himself the task of step two—taking the lead to build a temple for God. But at this point, God sovereignly stepped in to expand David's understanding about the way family callings work.

This intriguing Bible story is recorded in 1 Chronicles 22. God affirmed David's visionary accuracy and leadership initiative in making plans to build His house. But He reveals a missing ingredient in David's proposed strategy. The temple-building vision in David's heart was not for him to fulfill, but for his son, Solomon. God goes on to explain how the family calling flows from father to son.

David was called as a leader of war. Solomon was called as a leader of peace. On the surface, the two appeared to be extremely diverse. But in the design of God, the war and peace callings of father and son were vitally connected. The one flowed directly out of the other. As a leader-warrior, David laid the foundation for establishing the kingdom in peace. As a leader-ruler, Solomon was being raised up to build upon his father's foundation—building a house for the King of Peace.

This profound revelation for David literally revolutionized the way he approached the remainder of his life. Instead of focusing primarily on his own personal fulfillments, he now focused on being a way-maker for his son. The Bible indicates that "with great pains" and very costly investment, David devoted his energies to help Solomon fulfill the family leadership calling.

Even as Pop lacked perspective regarding family callings, I believe Dad saw through a glass darkly about this matter as well. I doubt that he ever gave much thought about the pioneering connection between his music and Pop's farming. Nevertheless, by faith and obedience, Dad was able to enter into the multi-generational lineage of Clemmer pioneers. I pray my generation and those that follow, each in their God-ordained way, may be graced to do the same thing.

12

Pioneering Prayer

Dad was a diligent student of his instrument. Something came alive deep inside as he sang and picked from those cowboy songbooks. With some of his spending money put aside over the months, he was able to upgrade from the beginner Stella model to an F-hole arch-top Metro Deluxe. The larger body style produced more volume, and his picking suddenly sounded more full and satisfying. The string action and neck were more comfortable to his hands, making the fingering of chords almost effortless. Dad's ear was developing as well. He began to hear fill-in notes, adding bass runs between the chord changes.

With the motivation of a true teacher, he immediately began developing a system to pass on these new play-by-ear extras to a few of his more advanced students. Between the chord-fingering diagrams above the melody line, Dad would pencil in symbols and write letter names of notes to be inserted as a melodic link between the chords of these well-worn tunes. In this time period of the 1930s, the only sheet music and songs written with chord symbols for guitar were cowboy ballads.

The evolution of the singing cowboy is an interesting American phenomenon. As the expansion of the United States moved westward during the 1800s, cattle quickly became big business. The figure of the robust, commanding cattlemen who rode with the cattle herds quickly emerged as a cultural icon. Americans became enthralled by the image of these cowboys.

Joe Clemmer, the "singin' Mennonite cowboy!"

Later, as theater and motion picture establishments began to flourish, it was only a matter of time before the entertainment business brought together the three facets—entertainer, cowboy, and singer. And in 1925, when Carl T. Sprague recorded the first cowboy hit "When the Work's All Done This Fall", the singing cowboy, as we know him, was born. Colorful figures such as Roy Rogers and Gene Autry produced a flurry of radio programs and movies featuring themselves with their horses and guitars. They became international celebrities, playing western ballads of the cowboy's life, his loves and his labors. Interest in guitar music mushroomed. Songbook collections of southern folk ballads and cowboy frontier tunes were published with fingering symbols for the guitar.

There was some sense of connection between the western cowboy and the eastern cattle-tending farmer. But for Dad, a conservative Mennonite, his life as a simple farmer was worlds apart from the gun-toting, guitar-picking, entertainer cowboy. Though this huge cultural gulf existed, Dad drank deeply from the wellspring of cowboy music. At the time, this was the only music resource affording him the opportunity to cultivate his own talent. He sang about "Birmingham Jail", "Red River Valley" and "The Big Rock Candy Mountain". Dad sang and taught cowboy songs, not because he identified experientially with the lyrics, but because his heart and soul were roused by playing the guitar to those tunes.

* * *

Dad loved springtime, and always gave himself whole-heartedly to working the ground. This year, plowing was an extra special treat. Pop had just purchased their first tractor, a Case with iron wheels. Dad especially looked forward to plowing the two fields at the far end of the farm next to the apple orchard. It seemed almost like another world, removed from the sight of any buildings or other signs of human activity.

The monotony of going back and forth across the fields along with the smell of freshly turned ground seemed to do a special number on his soul. Maybe it was the tilling of the earth that stimulated a similar kind of digging within the inner depths of his soul. This setting lifted out thoughts and feelings less likely to surface in the din of busy farm and family living. Dad thrived on the flurry of activity and industry generated to make the farm produce. But he welcomed the solitude and soul stimulus these secluded fields afforded.

It was a balmy day in mid April that Dad again found himself working that favorite plot of rolling ground in the back section. Drinking in the invigorating combination of spring air and freshly-plowed ground, his thoughts drifted back to the evening before.

Dad had been teaching one of his guitar students, a buddy who was really blossoming with musical ability. After the guitar lesson was over, they walked out to Dad's green Chevy, engrossed in mutually stimulating discussion. Dad and the student shared not only a love for the guitar, but also for the scriptures. Somewhere in the middle of their heart-to-heart talk, the subject of favorite hymns came up.

Floyd turned to Dad with a questioning look. "Are there any song-books that include sacred songs chorded for the guitar? It sure would be fun to pick church songs." Dad thought for a moment. "None that I know of," he responded. "I've been playing a few of my favorites like "What a Friend We Have in Jesus" and "Near the Cross" by ear, but I don't have a book with the chords. That sure would be great to have." The conversation had moved on without Dad giving it further thought, until now.

Dad made the turn at the end of the row. Heading back toward the far edge of the field, he began talking to himself. Was it possible that a book of hymns with guitar chords was in print? If so, how could he find out where to get one? As he continued down the row, another succession of questions bubbled to the surface. With the more simple hymns, he was able to hear and test out the proper chord changes by ear. Was there a way to actually analyze the chords from the soprano, alto, tenor and bass notes? If he could learn to figure out chords himself, there would be no need to purchase a published book with hymns and guitar diagrams.

An abrupt yank of the plow jagging on a rock quickly jolted Dad back to reality. Instantaneously, gripping and turning the wheel, he brought the plow back into line. Moments later, Dad resumed his previous train of thought. "Who could teach him the method to figure out how to chord hymns?" Finishing the last three rows of plowing, his mind kept persisting in its search for an answer to that haunting question. There was none to be found.

Dad pulled up the plow, shifted into neutral, and shut off the engine. After listening to the constant drone of the tractor for so long, its absence made the silence even more welcome. Gazing out across the unique beauty of those rich, brown furrows, a strange sensation began rising up from deep within. It was as though the question without answer was being transformed into a petition of simple request. "Lord, would you give me the understanding? Please God, show me how to figure out guitar chords for hymnbook songs. I need Your help." Though not verbalized aloud, the prayer was clearly articulated as a sincere cry from Dad's heart. God heard that prayer.

13

A Heart for Family

Mom rested her hands on her rounded belly. She could feel a gentle kick from the baby God had planted in her womb. Sitting at the kitchen table awaiting Dad's arrival for supper gave her a chance to rest between the mild contractions. She was eager to tell him of the labor pains that had begun a few hours earlier.

"What would it be like when the contractions got stronger?" she asked herself. Earlier that week, her mother had described the process of labor and delivery. She also recalled her mother saying that after the baby finally arrived the pain would be forgotten. How could that be, she wondered, as another wave of pain swept over her.

Just then Dad arrived home. "What's wrong?" he questioned, leaning down to give Mom a hug. "I've started having contractions a few hours ago. They're getting stronger but aren't very close together yet," she replied. "I'm glad I'm home," Dad responded, joining her at the table. Mom had prepared fresh strawberries and shortcake for supper. Mixed emotions of anticipation laced with anxiety had all but taken away their appetites.

That night Mom's contractions gradually increased in frequency and severity. In the early morning hours both agreed it was time to check in with Doc Jacobs. Doc was not only their family physician; he also owned the gentlemen's farm next door to the Alderfers. Several outbuildings on the same property provided a unique setting for Doc's medical offices and the small private hospital he managed. After listening to Mom describe the progress of her labor, Doc advised Dad to bring her to the hospital in preparation for delivery.

Upon arrival, Mom was escorted to the delivery room, where she invested several long hours of exhausting labor. The glorious payoff finally came later that morning as Mom held this long-awaited firstborn in her arms. With Mom and Dad's anniversary only three days away, Doris' safe arrival seemed to be a special gift to greatly enhance their upcoming celebration.

Meanwhile back at the Alderfer farm, Granddad was pacing up and down the barn hill. He was preoccupied with anxiety and fatherly concern for his daughter, Edith. How he wished for some news that could finally put his mind to rest. Because of his weakened heart condition, it was important that Granddad try as best he could to stay calm. Finally, the word came. How relieved he was when hearing the news his first grandchild had arrived and that the mother and baby were doing fine.

Previous to this, Mom had worked at Dexdale Hosiery in Lansdale. But now she was happy to stay at home with her new baby and assume the responsibilities of a full-time wife and mother. Days flew by. Before they knew it, Dad and Mom were hosting a one-year birthday party for their little girl. What a celebration it was with the Alderfer and Clemmer grandparents and a few aunts and uncles.

One sunny day Mom took Doris outside to enjoy the balmy summer weather. "My laundry will dry quickly today," she thought as she started hanging up the clothing from her overflowing basket. Suddenly glancing in the direction Doris had been playing, she realized that her little daughter was nowhere to be seen. With a panic-stricken voice she yelled, "Doris, come here!" Her command was met with a haunting silence. Not seeing her in the yard, Mom decided to search the neighboring corn field. Frantically weaving in and out among the high cornstalks, she cried out to God for help in finding her missing daughter.

Minutes seemed like hours as she continued her search. Suddenly she spied Doris' blue dress among the green stalks of corn. Catching up to her, Mom scooped Doris up in her trembling arms and carried her back to the yard. Breathing a sigh of relief, Mom thanked God for helping to find her runaway daughter in the huge corn maze.

* * *

Three years later Mother was carrying their second child. This time she knew a bit more about what to expect. Pregnancy and the signs of impending labor were more familiar to her now. Wednesday, September 18th, ten days before her due date, Mom started encountering mild labor pains. Caught by surprise, she continued monitoring the increased frequency and intensity of her contractions.

Dad explained the progress of Mom's labor to Dr. Albright. "It's too soon to go. I think she's having false labor," the doctor surmised. "Tell her to relax and take it easy," he added. However, Mom's labor continued to progress quite rapidly. In a short time she felt the need to push and gasped, "The baby is coming!" Severe birth pangs suddenly gave way to the miracle of birth. I [Janet] had the unique experience of entering the world in the privacy of my parents' bedroom.

In Psalm 70:6 David describes how God delivered him from his mother's womb. This was also true for me since no doctors or nurses were present at my birth. When asking Dad about this event the outstanding thing he remembered was the sight of Doctor Albright bounding up the steps to their bedroom. I'm sure he felt a great sense of relief after the doctor finally arrived. It is interesting to note that after this incident Mom and Dad decided to change doctors. Doc Wise served us for the remainder of our growing-up years. He not only attended to our medical needs, but ended up becoming a family friend and a beloved hunting buddy for Dad.

My parents intended to name me Joann, reflecting dad's name, Joe. However, his mother disliked that name, so they decided on Janet. The name was chosen from a story they had read about Doris and Janet.

My active nature, manifested in an early birth, was perpetuated as an adventuresome toddler. One day I ventured too close to the edge of the basement sump pump and fell in. Mom yelled when she saw what happened and quickly rescued me from the murky water. On another occasion when I was three years old, I stuck a curtain rod down my throat. Panic gripped Mom and Dad as they rushed me to Doc Wise. His exam confirmed that my throat and mouth had sustained significant damage. "We will have to admit Janet to the hospital and feed her intravenously," the doctor reported grimly. "How long will she have to stay?" Mom inquired tearfully. The doctor couldn't give an answer but indicated I would be there over the Christmas holidays.

Having a child in the hospital for the first time must have been a traumatic experience for Mom and Dad. They realized anew that life has its share of unexpected trials, but took this opportunity to again call upon the Lord as they had learned to do in the past.

* * *

Days and months went by and God blessed this couple with another gift from Heaven. As Mom went through her third pregnancy she wondered if this baby would be a boy or a girl. Before the days of ultrasounds, she could not know the answer to her question until the birth of her little one. Mom tired easily with two energetic youngsters to care for.

The last few weeks of waiting were tedious, but finally the time of birthing arrived. After a long wearying night, they notified Doc Wise and headed for Sellersville. The first rays of morning were appearing as Mom checked in at Grandview Hospital. On the bitter cold morning of December 20, 1942, they welcomed their first son into the family.

What a time of rejoicing it was. How exciting it was to have a son—the first grandson in both families. Numerous thoughts swirled back and forth in their tired minds. This one would carry on the Clemmer family name. Dad would have a boy to "rough house" with. The girls would have a brother. They were ecstatic!

In considering Dad and Mom's strong commitment to their Mennonite heritage, it is notable how they crossed denominational lines when choosing a name for their son. They named their first son after John and Charles Wesley, the Methodist pioneering preacher and songwriter team.

Doris and I adored our baby brother and became little mothers to him. Wesley was an active, inquisitive child. It was fun watching him explore his world. We made room for his trucks and tractors as they were added to our small collection of dolls and girl toys.

An amusing example of Wesley's exploration tendencies happened one day in an upstairs bedroom. Mom became absorbed in her cleaning, rushing to finish before the time to start dinner preparations. Suddenly she glanced up just in time to see her precious five-year-old son disappear over the sill of the upstairs window. Her mother heart raced wildly as she hurried downstairs, dreading to imagine the injuries he had sustained. "If only I had not left the window open," she lamented. Rushing down the porch steps, her anxious thoughts were interrupted when spying Wesley rounding the corner of the porch. He had landed in a bush instead of the hard ground and sustained only a few minor scratches and bruises. Though a bit shaken, he was fine. This event was mild in comparison to another accident Wesley experienced when he was ten years old.

* * *

It was a balmy April afternoon. After finishing his Saturday afternoon job of collecting eggs at the Clemmer homestead farm, it was time to head home. Mounting his bike, Wesley high-tailed it out the long graveled driveway. Riding bike and feeling the warm breeze blowing through his thick brown hair was invigorating. A large hedge of high bushes at the very end of the lane blocked his view of traffic traveling south on Rt. 113.

Without taking adequate time to stop and look, Wesley pulled out into the path of an oncoming car. The reverberation of screeching tires was immediately accompanied by the sickening sound of his bicycle being crunched underneath the car. Wesley was knocked unconscious, oblivious to what happened next.

After a few minutes, he gradually regained his senses, but struggled to grasp a sense of orientation. Lying on the back seat of a stranger's car, Wesley's attention was drawn to his left leg. It seemed to be twisted in an unnatural position. What had happened? Who was the man in the front seat? Where was he taking him? He felt puzzled, weak, and scared.

About that time, glancing in his rear view mirror, the driver noticed Wesley stirring. "What is your name? Where do you live?" the stranger quizzed. Aaron Swartz went on to fill in the pieces of what happened, informing Wesley they were on their way to Sellersville Hospital.

Finally they arrived at Grand View. An attendant quickly transported Wesley into the emergency room. Immediately someone placed a call to the house, informing Mom of the accident. Meanwhile, nurses and doctors took over and proceeded with their extensive examination. Aside from an assortment of superficial bruises and bumps, x-rays indicated Wesley's primary injury was a fractured left leg. In checking with admissions, it was discovered all pediatric rooms were filled. The only availability was in a twelve-bed men's ward.

Meanwhile, Mom was at home frantically attempting to locate Dad. He was winding up his Saturday afternoon teaching schedule. Finally, she made the connection. Upon receiving the shocking news, Dad rushed home. The whole family immediately sped to Grand View.

It was a tear-filled reunion as we all gathered around Wesley's bed. When I [Jan] first heard about his injury, I expected to see the broken leg in two pieces. Even though that wasn't the case, it was a traumatic experience observing his leg in traction. The maze of pipe framing, ropes and pulleys made the experience a bit unnerving.

Wesley remained in the men's ward for his entire six-week stay. This actually worked in his favor. Both the men patients and nurses gave him V.I.P. treatment, and Wesley happily accepted it. We made many hospital visits during those weeks of recuperation. This entire experience seemed to bond us closer together as a family.

Finally, Wesley was well enough to be discharged. How exciting it was to have him home again. Not being fond of school, he was delighted to have missed the last six weeks. Walking with crutches was a bit challenging, but he soon became adept at using them, quite happy to regain mobility.

* * *

God continued to fill Mom and Dad's quiver with select arrows. On April 18, 1944, we welcomed another sister. Lucille was a healthy baby and brought fresh joy to the family. However, at eighteen months she developed swollen glands, and for the next few years was frequently in and out of the hospital.

One day on the way to the hospital, Mom tearfully exclaimed to Dad, "I wish they would let me spend longer periods of time with Lucille. I wonder if we'll be bringing her home again." Hoping to encourage Mom he replied, "Let's keep trusting the Lord for her healing. God has helped us with the children's sicknesses in the past. I know He is with us in this one too."

Days of anxiety, intense prayer, and sleepless nights weighed upon Mom as she waited and hoped for healing and recovery. Gradually it became evident Lucille was improving. Finally the day came when they could bring her home. One more lesson in fighting the good fight of faith as parents would be put to good use, serving Dad and Mom for the rest of their married years.

* * *

Dean completed the family circle on July 5, 1950. Mother had lots of help since his older brother and sisters were usually close at hand. Previous to Dean's arrival, Wesley had frequently expressed his wish for a baseball glove and a brother. He finally had a brother. However, it would be several years before they could play baseball together.

We called Dean a "little live wire." Dad's home movies of Dean shaking the playpen humorously illustrate that fact. As an energetic and inquisitive toddler, he enjoyed exploring and learning about the world around him. More than once Dean wandered off into the woods behind our house, causing Mom no small amount of anxiety until he was finally found. Even though Dean came along several years behind the rest of us, he did a good job of keeping up with his siblings. Our family circle would have been incomplete without him.

These growing-up years were formative for us and also for Mom and Dad. The day-to-day experiences of raising a family taught them much about God and His intentions for Christ-honoring family living. Through the example of our parents, we have come to better understand the value of maintaining a heart for family. May we continually grow in that understanding!

*One of Dad's greatest joys—making music with his children.
Left to right: Wes, Janet, Lucy, Dad, Dean, and Doris, circa 1963.*

14

The Macedonian Call

Dad and Mom both inherited a strong sense of loyalty to their home Mennonite congregations. During the early months of 1936, in the midst of making wedding arrangements, they had begun exploring the question of which congregation should be their church home. It seemed quite logical to choose Mom's church. With their decision to set up housekeeping on the other side of the farmhouse with Mom's parents, Plains Mennonite would be less than a mile away.

On the other hand, there was a sense of desire on Dad's part to continue his involvement at Franconia. Being an outgoing sanguine personality, he had developed a number of close buddy relationships. These connections would be more easily maintained in the context of weekly church interaction. With his strong visionary motivation, Dad was not content merely riding along as a passive spectator. He thrived on being in the middle of the action. The large Franconia Church family would provide a wider variety of opportunities for ministry. Also, because of being a hub for the conference, Franconia's influence as a congregation extended to the other neighboring Mennonite churches. Its impact as a congregation was also felt in neighboring Lancaster Conference and beyond.

Therefore, in considering all the pros and cons, Dad felt the verdict was clear. It seemed reasonable to sink the roots of his marriage and emerging family into the rich soil at his home church. So it was settled. Franconia would be Dad and Mom's congregation.

Newly married, Dad invested himself in the work of the church. His musical ability as chorister provided a logical position where he could contribute. But Dad was also strongly motivated to keep scanning the horizon for other ministry work. He was drawn to opportunities that included a frontier dimension—work that required foundation-laying gifts. Though not consciously thinking in these terms, Dad was being stirred to exercise his calling in the spirit of a true pioneer.

At the same time, there was a fresh pioneering spirit being awakened within the larger Mennonite church. A new sense of call to mission outreach was being felt within Franconia Conference. Those with evangelistic motivation began experiencing an urgency to impact outlying areas with practical Christian witness.

One of these outreaches grabbed Dad's attention. The invitation came through a successful Mennonite businessman from Harleysville. Arthur Lapp was a bundle of energy, active not only in his flourishing poultry business, but also as a visionary mover and shaker in the church.

Arthur had stopped by the farm one day to talk with Pop, but he had gone to town. Dad and Arthur began chatting about poultry prices, Harry Price's recent expansion of the Harleysville Poultry Auction, and other farm-related business. Eventually the conversation switched to church matters. He and some other local mission-minded men from area congregations were driving to Norristown once a month to distribute evangelistic Christian pamphlets door-to-door.

"Joe, you oughta go with us!" Arthur exclaimed with a note of excitement in his voice. "It means getting up early, but that way it doesn't interfere with getting to church." "Yea, I'd like to do that," Dad offered in reply. This opportunity for exercising his faith in a new environment resonated within Dad, and he began to participate in the outreach. The group of guys left from home very early Sunday morning and traveled thirty miles to the Norristown Mennonite Mission. *The Way* distribution was a strategy to impact city households in close proximity to the mission with the Gospel.

These workers from larger outlying congregations partnered with the small core group of on-site mission workers. Approximately thirty to forty gathered together for a short devotional and time of prayer before hitting the streets. Bundled packets with current editions of *The*

Way pamphlets were handed out to the workers. Each team drove a short distance to their assigned streets and began the distribution, two by two. Afterward, everyone returned home in time to attend their regular Sunday morning church services.

This opportunity to interact with other men who had a heart for expanding the influence of the church was a positive stimulus for Dad. He was inspired by these leaders who took their faith seriously. The sense of fellowship and teamwork experienced in the Norristown outreach was a newfound joy. It was also formative in helping Dad better understand the unique challenges of ministering to people "on the other side of the tracks."

One eye-opening experience happened when Dad and Wayne Martin were grouped together. Their assignment consisted of a few streets near the river, on the "rough" side of town. Moving methodically from door to door, they were suddenly aware of a man running up to them. He was quite conspicuous, "all dirty and smeared up." Almost out of breath, he blurted out, "Where is the Catholic church? I must see the priest!"

Both Dad and Wayne attempted to calm him down, all the while pressing him for more information. A bit more composed but still somewhat confused, the stranger modified his request. "Take me to the police station."

About this time, two other fellows from the mission returned who were to pick up Dad and Wayne. Together, they escorted the deranged man to their car. Positioning this stressed-out guy between them in the back seat, they sped away to the police station. What a foul-smelling ride!

When they arrived at the station and presented their passenger, pieces of his story began falling into place. The man was a runaway from the Norristown mental hospital, and had escaped through a large sewage pipe. That accounted for the slime and stench. A manhunt had already been organized, so the police were quite happy for Dad and Wayne's help in apprehending this missing escapee.

Though a bit unnerving and beyond their ministry assignment, Wayne and Dad did get rewarded with a bit of unexpected publicity. When the news account broke, it applauded "the two church boys who were distributing *The Way* gospel tracts" as the courageous captors. But beyond the payoff of short-lived excitement and notoriety, both men reaped a much greater reward. Dad and Wayne were being sensitized at a deeper level to the hurts and needs of broken people. They returned home with a renewed motivation for ministry extending beyond the confines of their wholesome rural communities.

During World War II, gasoline rationing made it necessary to make adjustments to the schedule and transportation arrangements for the monthly Norristown distributions. It was decided that moving the outreach to Sunday afternoon would be more economical. Men from the Franconia area could carpool to the Souderton station, and ride the trolley to Norristown. This was a permanent change, and the Sunday afternoon distribution continued into the 1960s. Dad helped in this Norristown distribution for over twenty years. Some of us children eventually participated as well.

* * *

In those first years of *The Way* distribution, one of the men who traveled regularly to Norristown with Dad was Titus Metz. Titus was an older man from a neighboring congregation who had been an active church worker for many years. During the course of those early Sunday morning rides together, Titus and Dad developed a growing sense of respect and appreciation for one another.

It was while returning home on a trip from Norristown near the end of a lively discussion that Titus turned to Dad. His voice shifted to a more serious tone. "Joe, we're struggling with the work at Towamencin. We could really use a few Sunday school teachers, and the singing lacks spirit and enthusiasm. Maybe a big part of the problem is that we need some new life in the place."

Titus paused a moment, and then looked straight at Dad. "Would you and Edith consider coming to Towamencin to help us? Franconia has plenty of helpers; more than they can really put to work. It would be such a blessing if you could be released to come and lend us a hand."

Dad was moved by the intensity of the appeal. He had heard the Towamencin congregation was going through some difficulties, but was taken off guard by this invitation from Titus. Thoughts and questions began to run around in his mind. Dad felt honored that Titus placed this kind of confidence in him. Yet, to leave Franconia would be a huge step. What would Pop and Mum say? Would Edith be open to the move? If this seemed like a change they were to make, it would need to be processed with and approved by the ministers at Franconia.

"I don't know, Titus. Give me some time to think about it. Edith and I are committed at Franconia, but I wanna be open," Dad paused again, not sure what else to say. In silence, Titus waited. "Let me work on this, Titus, and I'll get back to you. I guess I'd be willing to give it a try if Edith is agreed and the ministers at Franconia release me." Titus grinned. "That's fair enough, Joe."

Later that morning as Dad and Mom were headed down the Allentown Road on their way home from church, he began sharing with Mom about the unexpected invitation from Titus. After finishing the story, Dad turned to Mom with his quizzical grin. "Well, whatdaya think? Should we consider it?" Mom's look was hard to read. "Joe, we really felt that our place was at Franconia. It is true what Titus said. I guess I'm willing to consider going if you believe that's what we should do."

By this time they had made the turn onto Troxel Road, and a few moments later were pulling up to the house. As they shut the car door and headed down the long walk to the back door, Dad broke the silence. "Edie, it kinda sounds like the Macedonian call from the man in the Apostle Paul's dream, doesn't it? If we were to say yes to this appeal, we might be able to really make a difference. It would be good to see Towamencin become a stronger congregation again." Mom nodded. "That would certainly be our hope," she responded. "Maybe when you share this with the leaders at Franconia, the way they respond will help us know what to do."

Later, when Dad discussed the opportunity with Pastor Menno Souder, Menno was objective in his response. "Yes, Joe, I know Towamencin has been struggling for quite some time. If you and Edith would leave Franconia, that would be a loss for us." Menno glanced down for a moment, and then back to Dad. "Yet, we want to be a help to others when we can. That's what the church is all about. Let me run this by a few of the other brothers and I'll get back to you with an answer." "Okay," Dad replied. "I'll wait to hear from you."

It was a few weeks before Dad got the word from Menno. His response was favorable—they affirmed the move. Dad and Mom interpreted the blessing from the Franconia leaders as a sign this invitation was indeed a genuine Macedonian call—the will of the Lord. It was decided they would maintain their church membership at Franconia, but regularly attend and be involved with the work at Towamencin.

* * *

Dad eagerly rolled up his sleeves, giving himself without reservation to his first assignment at Towamencin—a lively Sunday school class of teenage boys. Keeping these energetic fellows reigned in was a handful, but Dad's quick mind and wit served him well. He took a genuine interest in his pupils. They began responding positively to his engaging class discussions.

Preparing weekly to teach launched Dad into a new discipline of biblical study and research. He had been a regular reader of the Bible ever since his salvation experience. Now, with this weekly teaching responsibility, Dad was motivated to dig deeper in his personal study of the Word. Being busy with the farm work and guitar teaching didn't leave much time for study during the week. So, early Sunday morning became the most ideal time to prepare for teaching his weekly lesson.

Gifted as a teacher, Dad's interest in mining out the truths and presenting these insights became an ever-increasing personal delight. This enjoyment colored his teaching. Dad taught with consistent enthusiasm, and the boys sat up and listened.

In addition to the class assignment, Dad's contribution as a song leader was an immediate blessing to the congregation. Unlike many choristers of his day, Dad's song leading was strengthened by his ongoing study of music theory and dynamics. For him, it was not a matter of merely singing the hymn, but instead being in touch with and interpreting the expressive dimensions of tempo, dynamics, harmonies and message.

During a large portion of those early years at Towamencin, the church sang from two different songbooks. One of these, *The Church and Sunday School Hymnal*, was a standard in the Mennonite churches of that era. The hymnal was issued in 1902 and compiled under the direction of J. D. Brunk from the Virginia Conference. Assisting J.D. was a committee of church music people appointed by other Mennonite conferences across the nation. It contained a huge assortment of over 500 hymns and gospel songs, many that became Dad's favorites.

Dad detested passive and lifeless congregational singing. Being a tall man with a strong voice, he had not only the heart but also the physical attributes to encourage active, enthusiastic participation with his leading. He led with spirit, and people responded.

As Dad grew in his leading experience, he became more sensitive in making song selections appropriate for particular applications—opening songs, closing songs, and the like. He especially enjoyed leading the majestic and big-sounding hymns, regularly using them to begin services. "All Hail the Power of Jesus' Name" was the first song in the hymnal, and one of his favorite opening numbers.

Though many song leaders in that era used a tuning fork, Dad preferred the newer multi-toned pitch pipe. A little inner pocket in his suit coat was designed for pocket watches. It also provided an excellent place for Dad to keep his pitch pipe.

Another chorister who served in the song leader rotation was Alvin Keeler. Alvin, an elderly gentlemen, used the old-fashioned fork. Abe Allebach was a bit closer to Dad's age. Together, these three occupied the second to front bench and took turns leading each Sunday. Years later as Alvin and Abe became too old to serve, other choristers took their places.

When I [Wes] was about five or six, Dad decided I was old enough to sit between him and Alvin on the "chorister's bench." As I recall, this felt like a privilege, but it also presented a unique challenge. Being on the second front bench and within full view of the congregation, I had to sit reasonably still. This became especially tedious when the sermon went into overtime or dealt with biblical truth that was "over my head."   Fortunately, I had two life-saving diversions that helped me endure. One of these was actually a form of entertainment. Tricky-dogs. I am hard pressed to remember if it was Alvin or Abe who owned the engaging creatures. But with Dad's permission, those two little black and white one-inch magnetic dogs were passed to me. I was able to amuse myself for extended periods of time, all the while appearing well behaved to the congregation viewing only the top of my head. Even the preacher must have been impressed with my apparent attentiveness to his preaching.

The other diversion was helpful in quite a different way. These choristers were always well supplied with an essential aid for their music ministry—throat-soothing lozenges to keep their voices clear. The throat drop of choice at the time was Helps. Though quite small, these little coal-black Helps were actually quite potent with a good bit of tang to their taste.

About halfway into the sermon, one of the choristers would reach into his side coat pocket. I instantly knew what was coming. He would pull out the familiar little red and yellow box, slide back the cover, and pass it down the line of choristers for all to partake. Though I was not yet an official member in the chorister lineup, I was granted the privilege of taking a few Helps to keep my throat clear as well. It felt like a true manly privilege, and brought a sense of enjoyment and affirmation to my boyhood church experience at Towamencin.

15

Peer Pioneers

The initial move to Towamencin had a certain tentativeness about it. But meaningful relational connections quickly bonded Dad and Mom with the congregation. Within a short time their sense of call to this church family was confirmed as a permanent one.

A few years after Dad and Mom's arrival, an unexpected development thrust the congregation into a new chapter of challenge and change. Isaac Kulp, aging preacher and failing in health, requested a release from his position as minister. Isaac was an effective leader. He and Warren Moyer, the other minister, had served well together and been compatible as a leader team. An obvious question loomed in the hearts of the membership. Who would the Lord raise up to move Towamencin forward in this time of crucial transition?

The year was 1939. For the Mennonite church of that day, standard practice for identifying a new leader was the biblical procedure of "the lot." The first chapter of Acts provides a scriptural precedent for this selection process. When identifying the need to replace Judas, the disciple-betrayer of Christ, the remaining disciples of Jesus nominated two men as qualified candidates. After praying to God for direction in the choosing process, they cast lots—drew straws, so to speak. Through this action, Matthias was authorized to serve alongside the other eleven as the replacement apostle.

In Mennonite doctrine, the belief that divine providence sovereignly controlled who received the lot was based on Proverbs 16:33. "The lot is cast into the lap, but the whole disposing thereof is of the

Lord." To begin the course of action, names were solicited from adult church members. These nominations identified men the congregation felt would be qualified to shepherd the flock.

Three candidates, Abram Metz, Jr., Isaac Alderfer, and Howard Hackman were identified. These men were looked upon as seasoned pillars of the church and capable of providing spiritual leadership. A fourth nominee, Bill Anders, was in a very different category—a young man in his early twenties. He had just returned home a few weeks earlier as a graduate from Eastern Mennonite College in Harrisonburg, Virginia.

Bill was a native son, having grown up in the Towamencin church family. As a young man, Bill's sense of call to the foreign mission field was the igniting spark of inspiration prompting him to seek ministry preparation at EMC. Upon his graduation, Bill was not yet clear where his missionary calling was to be fulfilled. He had returned home, but was now confronted with this unexpected ministry opportunity as a nominee for the lot.

A special ordination service was called for Tuesday morning, June 20th. The significance of this event attracted many other interested community folk, resulting in an overflow crowd. Every church bench and extra wooden folding chair was occupied. A sizable group was forced to stand and listen to the lengthy service from outside.

Bishop Arthur Ruth of Line Lexington officiated. At least two other Franconia Conference bishops participated in the service. Even the neighboring Lancaster Conference was represented. Bishop John Sauder and Bishop Noah Landis preached back-to-back sermons as a featured part of the ordination event. At the appointed time, four identical hymnals were taken by Bishop Ruth, shuffled, and then set up, side by side, on the pulpit. Each contained a slip of paper, but only one had the Proverbs 16:33 verse written upon it.

Everyone felt the growing sense of anticipation as each candidate solemnly walked to the pulpit and selected a book. In no heart was the concern of the moment felt more intensely than within these four men. Each in turn opened the hymnal he chose. These books represented such a common part of their weekly worship experience. But on this occasion, holding and opening the songbook felt radically different.

The contents of this hymnal could dictate a potential directive that would radically alter their life. This assignment would not only change the candidate's personal life, but drastically impact the future of his wife and generational offspring.

Young Bill Anders was the last to choose. Sure enough, Bill's hymnal contained the scripture-inscribed slip of paper tucked between its pages. With a young visionary minister now a part of the leadership team, the congregation was being providentially postured for significant change.

* * *

Without any strong feeling, Bill accepted the verdict as a sovereign directive from God for his future. He willingly picked up the baton to assist Warren Moyer as a minister at Towamencin. This appointment to serve as a local church preacher was totally unexpected. It seemed far removed from his sense of call as a foreign missionary. Though lacking a tangible sense of confirmation within himself, Bill chose to step forward in faith. He believed the call to obedience as higher than following the fickleness of feelings or a dimly defined vision. Somehow, God would eventually make sense out of this mystifying "turn in the road."

Dad was elated by Bill's ordination. Their relationship deepened quickly, nurtured by a rich sense of being drawn alongside one another as compatible friends. A common love for deer hunting made them instant hunting buddies. Several other young married fellows from Towamencin were also avid hunters, and together they connected with a small gang of hunters from neighboring communities. These guys had been hunting in the rugged forests of central Pennsylvania near Orviston, a little mining town at the end of the road. Bill and Dad fit right in. Their yearly hunts as members of the Poor Shot Hunting Club provided an ideal setting to stir up the fun-loving side of their sanguine personalities. Fun and humor are great uniting agents. In the context of these annual prank-filled hunting trips, Dad and Bill nurtured their sense of friendship and brotherhood.

But recreation was only one of the uniting factors. Bill was also a good singer. Their common interest in music offered yet another way for them to interact. Inspired by Dad's music and love for the guitar, Bill purchased a guitar and began taking lessons. Dad quickly walked him though the beginner book of notes and scales. Bill was a quick learner, and it wasn't long until Dad had pulled out the hymnbook and chorded a few of their favorites. Bill and his wife, Miriam, had great voices, and were known for their rich, close-harmony duet sound. Now, with the addition of Bill's guitar, their singing was enhanced. Of course, Bill and Miriam still sang acappella in church settings, but added the guitar whenever their singing assignment took them outside those four walls. They became one of Dad's greatest encouragers.

It took only a short time for Bill's preaching gifts to be recognized. As he became established as a leader at Towamencin, the people enthusiastically responded to his life-giving messages. This communication gift coupled with Bill's passion to lead the church forward was a winning combination. Under the complimentary partnership of seasoned Warren Moyer and dynamic Bill Anders, the congregation transitioned into a brand new season of health and numerical growth.

Though initially less obvious, Dad and Bill's emerging sense of partnership in ministry was to be the greatest uniting factor in their relationship. Working with Bill in ministry was a new treat for Dad. He respected Isaac Kulp and Warren Moyer as ministers, but their approaches to church work were shaped by perspectives of the passing generation. They seemed content to maintain the status quo. In contrast, Bill shared Dad's passion for progressive thinking and pursuing new frontiers.

It would be interesting to know if both men recognized the common ingredient of pioneering spirit they shared while pouring themselves into the work at Towamencin. Each was a special gift to the other. Over time, a unique spiritual bonding manifested on Sundays when Dad led singing and Bill preached. This harmony of spirit seemed to release what Psalm 133 addresses—a unique blessing commanded by the Lord upon those who dwell (and partner) together in unity.

Though not blood brothers like John and Charles Wesley, their partnership in preaching and praise bore some similar resemblance. Dad's lively singing inspired Bill's preaching, and Bill's exhortations fueled Dad's song leading. Partnering with Bill was, no doubt, one of the most fulfilling seasons of Dad's fifty years as a church worker at Towamencin.

* * *

Pioneers gravitate to other pioneers. Another unique friendship that developed with a fellow pioneer in the Mennonite church was with Gerald Derstine. Gerald was a bit younger than Dad, and grew up in the neighboring Souderton congregation. Though schooled in the acappella preferences of the church, Gerald also found himself being drawn to instrumental music. He was especially attracted to the accordion. As a teen, Gerald chose to contact a music studio in Lansdale for lessons. With a natural ear for music, Gerald quickly developed as a gifted musician.

He chuckles while telling the story of what happened when wanting to buy his first car. Right before making the purchase, Gerald heard about a 120-bass accordion for sale at a reasonable price. His was a smaller model, so this sounded like a tempting offer. With limited finances, he could not purchase both the car and the accordion. While weighing out the pros and cons of both items, Gerald decided the normal upkeep of a vehicle would continue costing him money. In contrast, the accordion would only cost him the initial purchase price. It seemed like a no-brainer. He bought the accordion.

Because of their similar pursuits, an eventual connection between Dad and Gerald was inevitable. As fellow Mennonites with a love for instrumental music, a bond quickly formed. They began getting together for the sheer delight of making music. These jam sessions provided a different outlet for Dad. Gerald was not a student, but more of a peer. Therefore, Dad could lay down his teacher role and enjoy teaming with another accomplished musician.

At the time Dad had a new recorder that produced home recordings. This was advanced technology for that day. The recorder would actually cut grooves on a blank disc producing a seven-inch record playable on any 78 RPM record player. I have several of those records he recorded, one with a Motorola label and the song "All For Me" by Joe and Jerry. This good-sounding duo never exported their music, but they should have. The bond with Gerald formed during those music-making sessions had to be one of the great enjoyments of Dad's life.

After Gerald was married, he and Beulah responded to an invitation from his uncle, Lewelyn Groff, to help with a mission outreach among Native Americans in northern Minnesota. Gerald's accordion music was an effective tool in connecting with the youth. He also began providing leadership for a Bible study consisting of hungry new believers. As this group continued to meet, they began shifting their focus to praying for revival. God answered their prayers in an unusual way. This fascinating story has been written in a book by Gerald and his daughter, *Following The Fire*.

One evening, near the end of 1955, this group experienced a sovereign spiritual visitation with unusual manifestations that were first interpreted as not being from God. Having never experienced anything like this before, Gerald attempted to rebuke evil spirits, believing they were responsible for these unfamiliar demonstrations. When this proved unsuccessful, he was made to realize this was indeed a present work of God. The unusual happening seemed to mirror the biblical account of Pentecost in the book of Acts.

It was not long before the reports of a supernatural visitation traveled back to Gerald's home congregation in Souderton. Instantly this news became the talk of the local Mennonite community. Without a framework of doctrinal understanding and openness to accept the unexplainable, it was generally interpreted as "Gerald having gone off the deep end."

When Dad got wind of this, he was hard pressed to be critical or judgmental of Gerald. Though not fully understanding or being able to explain what was being reported, Dad knew Gerald's heart. In communicating his personal position on the matter, Dad would always say, "We need to be cautious and not quick to criticize those we don't understand. Time itself will help to clarify the truth. Meanwhile, we need to pray and be supportive of our brothers and sisters, even though we may not agree with or understand them." What wisdom. Twenty years later, Gerald was invited back to his home congregation. Finally the church was able to validate his call as a spiritual pioneer to his generation.

Dad maintained a sense of loyalty to Gerald through the years. They had ongoing opportunities to nurture their friendship when Gerald would return to the community for family visits. Years later, when Gerald moved to Bradenton, Florida, to establish Christian Retreat Center as his international ministry base, Dad and Mom began making yearly visits to CRC. These times of connection were always treasured, providing occasion for Gerald and Dad to reminisce.

They reflected on the ways God had allowed them to enrich one another's lives as fellow pioneers in diverse fields—Dad fulfilled his pioneering within the confines of the Mennonite church, and Gerald plowed new ground as a missionary, well beyond the fences erected by his religious forefathers. In the midst of it all, the gift of brotherhood and partnership between Dad and Gerald was so honorably expressed. It has provided an inspirational model for us children. What a priceless treasure.

16

The Test of Fellowship

I have no knowledge of Bill Anders and Gerald Derstine ever spending much time together. It seems ironic, especially because these two pioneers were close to Dad and both had passionate missionary hearts. Bill's missionary heart, though not activated in the context of another ethnic community or culture, was functional nonetheless. As the saying goes, "a person's gifts make room for them." This was certainly confirmed in Bill's developing ministry while at Towamencin.

Making friends and endearing himself to those outside the faith came natural to Bill. It strengthened his effectiveness as a church leader. But this motivation to influence and include outsiders beyond the confining Mennonite boundaries would prove to undermine what otherwise could have been a long tenure for him at Towamencin. One example of how this outreach motivation worked against Bill is vividly illustrated in the following account involving an "outsider."

An older man from the community had become a convert and sought out Bill about being baptized and becoming a member at Towamencin. In those days, accepting outsider converts as candidates for membership was not very common in the older traditional congregations. It did happen more frequently in the newer mission outreaches of the church. Outsiders were approved as candidates, contingent upon their readiness to affirm and live out the church doctrines.

Though some of the Mennonite requirements for membership involved matters of the heart, much weight was placed upon embracing the accepted dress code for men and women. These spelled-out rules varied a bit from conference to conference, but always upheld the firm conviction of separation from the world. Church leaders of the day usually stressed non-conformity to the world as a primary evidence of genuine heart repentance. Failing to conform outwardly would raise serious questions about the sincerity of a person's heart.

This convert who approached Bill seemed to evidence a genuine turnaround in his life, except for one conspicuous thing—his mustache. Without the benefit of an inborn cultural conviction or understanding, removing his mustache seemed to be an unreasonable requirement. To this novice in the faith, conforming seemed to be more man-pleasing than God-honoring. Why couldn't he be baptized with his mustache? He refused to remove it.

Bill felt caught in the middle. Realizing how easily the church's letter-of-the-law approach could become a stone of stumbling, he felt compelled to take this matter to the bishop and make the reasonable appeal. Regarding externals, certainly there should be some allowances made for outsiders who are spiritual infants. As Bill understood it, inner transformation eventually produces external transformation. Genuine change happens from the inside out. God had certainly begun a good work in this man, and He would be faithful to continue the life-changing process.

It was from this point of view that Bill presented his appeal. In fact, he made multiple visits, certain the bishop would eventually understand. But there was no budging. If the candidate refused to comply, there would be no baptism. Bill's evangelistic heart was crushed.

Fortunately, the baptism did eventually take place, all because the man was finally willing to remove his mustache. But this episode deeply impacted Bill, etching abrasions in the form of haunting question marks within his heart. These questions would continue to fester and grow in the coming months and years. How could the passion burning in his heart to reach the unchurched be fulfilled within a religious system that imposed cultural law upon Christ-seekers? Could Towamencin truly be the place God had called him to invest these priority fruit-bearing years of his life?

Did the Mennonite doctrine of non-conformity, as it was practically spelled out, really contribute to the life and witness of Christ as He intended it to be expressed across the cultures? What was God really calling him to pursue as a minister? What about his missionary vision?

From time to time, Bill's internal questions spilled over. Because of their deep friendship, Dad was one of those close at hand to offer a listening ear. Whether in the midst of a deer hunting excursion or during a visit between our families, Bill would share his heart and Dad would serve as his sounding board.

Dad certainly shared a lot of Bill's sentiments. A good number of his music students were not Mennonites. Many had a vibrant faith, lived out in the context of various denominational persuasions. Though professing heart-felt Christian belief, these students certainly would have been in violation of Mennonite dress standards. But without question, numbers of these gave a genuine witness as true followers of Christ. Dad saw no reason and made no effort to indoctrinate them. He agreed with Bill. "In essentials unity; in non-essentials liberty; in everything, charity." Within the context of Dad's ministry out in the marketplace, this conviction released him. But in the context of Bill's ministry within the Mennonite church, this conviction was causing him to be misunderstood.

* * *

Years passed, and Bill's tenure stretched into the mid-1940s—an era of radical change. Rapidly developing media advances and increased global awareness triggered by World War II had a profound effect upon the western church of that day. It was as if a slumbering giant had awakened. Many denominations caught a renewed sense of vision for outreach and propagating their faith throughout the world. New church mission agencies were formed and existing ones reignited. Not only did this renewal involve a new commitment to foreign missions, but a number of churches were motivated to become more outreach oriented, intent on impacting the lives of unbelievers in their local regions.

A segment of Mennonites were included in this "witness wave," birthing mission works both at home and abroad. But many of the large traditional congregations struggled to genuinely embrace the new paradigm of evangelism. Individuals in these congregations with a heart for outsiders became frustrated when their attempts to promote outreach were rebuffed. Verbal belief in the Great Commission was generally affirmed by leaders. They raised no argument with the scriptural command. But often these same leaders were reluctant to make room in the congregational fold for black sheep—strangers with different cultural backgrounds and sordid histories. It felt too much like compromise. If people couldn't measure up to the standard, why should they be fully included and endorsed in the brotherhood?

As an evangelistically motivated leader, Bill had a genuine love for black sheep. Like the sons of Issachar as mentioned in the Bible, he had an understanding of the times and what the church was being called to. Bill was also strategically positioned to launch this "inclusion" vision and move the congregation forward. But with successive attempts, it soon became obvious that Towamencin was not yet ready to move this direction. As time wore on, Bill became increasingly frustrated by this deadlock. What should he do?

It was an agonizing process, but after months of travail in prayer, Bill and Miriam finally made their decision to resign. Reluctance and expectancy were intermingled in their resignation statement—reluctant to sever meaningful ties with a congregation they dearly loved; expectant for the future and the sense of call to fulfill God's expanding missional purposes for their life.

Bill's resignation announcement sent shock waves throughout the congregation. This was especially traumatic for two reasons. Minister Warren Moyer, who had served Towamencin for thirty-two years, had passed away only six months earlier. Still grieving from the loss of this beloved long-term leader, the news of Bill's leaving was all the more difficult to accept.

In reality, this would not leave them totally leaderless. Sunday School teacher, Ellis Mack, had been recently ordained as minister to assist Bill after Warren's death. But it would naturally take some additional time for Ellis to earn the place of respect that only comes with years of proven service with a congregation.

The second reason that caused the church great concern related to Bill's intensions upon leaving Towamencin. At the time of his resignation, Bill also shared plans to begin a non-denominational church in a neighboring community. The vision clearly articulated what had been in Bill's heart all along—to build a church with a heart and focus to impact the unchurched of that area. If this value was instilled in the foundation-laying stage, Bill was convinced his vision could be accomplished.

There were a good number of Bill's Towamencin peers who resonated with his pioneering aspirations. But to the congregation as a whole, it felt like a divorce, and painfully familiar. Five years earlier, there had been a similar departure of a sizable group. That exodus gave birth to Grace Bible Church in nearby Souderton. It was propagated by doctrinal disagreements about eternal security and end-time theology. During that time, Bill had attempted to serve as a bridge between the Conference and those in disagreement. But his efforts were unsuccessful in preventing the split.

Now, Bill's decision to leave and begin a new congregation was easily interpreted as another round of rejection and betrayal. Families and individuals would be forced to choose—either to remain loyal to the church and their Mennonite heritage, or to leave and align themselves with the departing leader. Inevitably, this would trigger division in long-standing relationships, and even within families.

Dad and Mom, especially because of their close friendship with Bill and Miriam, were thrust into the middle of this emotional whirlpool. In many ways, Dad and others resonated with Bill's pioneering vision and would be motivated to follow. Yet, Dad still felt a strong sense of commitment to his ministry assignment at Towamencin. He also shared Mom's heart connection with the church family.

Through the years, Dad had gained a lot of favor with the entire church. His investment as an engaging Sunday School teacher and dynamic song leader was vitally impacting the life of the congregation. Dad felt fulfilled in his place. Yet, at times, he was frustrated with the church for not allowing musical instruments to have a place in worship. Going with Bill could open up this door. It was all so confusing. What should he do? What would be best for the family? What was God saying? How could he and Mom truly know God's will?

In those days that followed, wrestling intensely in this valley of decision, Dad confided and sought advice from a variety of friends. A close buddy, Hiram, was one person with a lot of wisdom from whom Dad especially wanted to seek counsel. Hiram had many of the same connections with Bill as Dad. It would be easy for him to be objective. Dad put the question to Hiram straight on. "What should I do?" Wisely, Hiram responded, "I can't tell you what to do. You've got to hear and obey what God tells you to do." Though Dad didn't want to hear it, he knew Hiram's answer was right.

Lessons designed by God to develop our spiritual hearing and discernment are usually administered within the framework of crisis, conflict, and change. We labor to sort out or separate the whisperings of our own heart from the still, small voice of the Lord. Fortunately, sincere seeking and humble waiting bring their due rewards.

Oddly enough, the final decision that ultimately surfaced in Dad was not the most reasonable one. In the natural, there appeared to be significantly more reasons to go with Bill than to stay. But Dad and Mom finally came into agreement—to remain at Towamencin. They had been called to this place. There was a clear sense of this being an assignment from the Lord. For some strange reason, that assignment was not yet completed.

With heavy hearts, Dad and Mom communicated their decision with Bill and Miriam. Tears and strong verbal affirmations of love confirmed a mutual desire to continue building upon the foundation of friendship that had become so life-giving and precious. This commitment expressed between them that day was admirably lived out through the remaining years of their lives. Even so, the departure was heart-wrenching.

The launch service of Calvary Church took place at the Telford Fire Hall on March 25, 1950. Bill preached his initial message to over 100 attendees. A year later, the congregation began building on property purchased along Route 113, just outside Souderton.

* * *

Bill and Miriam pastored Calvary Church for ten years. Under their able leadership, the congregation enjoyed significant growth, vitally impacting the greater North Penn Valley. A strong outreach vision enabled the church to quickly become a vital supporter of foreign missions. They resourced and supported missionary couples and families around the world. More recently, the church has been very effective in raising up missionaries from within the church, sowing their own members and launching ministries into other communities and foreign countries.

Upon completing their pastoral ministry at Calvary, Bill and Miriam were released and sent out to fulfill their original missionary dream. Upon completion of their state-side jungle school training, the Anders moved to Ecuador and served a term of several years working among the tribal Natives of this needy South American country.

After Bill and Miriam left Towamencin, Dad and Bill always enjoyed the opportunity to reconnect on their yearly deer-hunting expeditions. Our families continued to visit back and forth, though not with the frequency enjoyed during the Towamencin days. Underneath all of these outward gestures of ongoing friendship was the inward sense that, though serving on different teams, they could genuinely support and honor one another in their common pursuit of Kingdom advancement.

* * *

During the challenging season that followed Bill and Miriam's departure, Dad and others at Towamencin began sacrificially investing themselves in the vital rebuilding process. It was slow-going. Many of those who had been active workers and liberal in investing themselves had moved on. Now there were fewer workers to shoulder the load.

Young families were not as well represented anymore. With a shortage of children workers and a smaller number of pupils, the Sunday School department needed a significant shot in the arm. It seemed obvious that a vibrant ministry to children would help strengthen the congregation and could also attract new families.

During this time, other churches in the Franconia Conference were exploring new ways of impacting children, mainly through the ministry of summer Bible schools. Several church plants in urban areas outside Mennonite communities used summer Bible schools as an effective way to initiate outreach. As the congregation developed a meaningful connection with the children, it provided a vital link to building relationships with their parents.

Using this as a point of reference, the Towamencin leaders began discussing how they could institute a similar approach in targeting community kids. Though having some vague knowledge about the philosophy of summer Bible school outreaches, no one in the circle felt capable of directing the effort. Possibly someone from the Conference could help put the pieces of this puzzle together for them.

In answer to this plea for help, Richard Detweiler was enlisted to help launch the first Towamencin summer Bible school. At the time, Richard pastored Perkasie Mennonite Church. He was also gaining recognition at the Conference level. Richard was a strong leader, uniquely gifted as both a passionate visionary and wise administrator. Towamencin was very fortunate to have Richard at the helm of their new outreach venture.

Stirred by this pioneering opportunity, Dad agreed to serve as Richard's assistant. Part of the attraction was having the opportunity to lead the children's singing for each daily opening session. He welcomed the challenge to develop a repertoire of songs that kids would enjoy. This connected directly to Dad's passion for investing musically in the next generation.

Advertising and word-of-mouth solicitation made the community kids aware of what was coming. Teachers were recruited, and materials were purchased. Everything came together, and the Bible school was launched. Sessions were held each morning, Monday through Friday, for two weeks.

Dad's song leading was one of the significant highlights for the kids. Many of the choruses he chose included hand and body motions, catchy tunes, and fun lyrics. Dad had the great ability to exhort children to move beyond their inhibitions and sing with gusto. At times, he would divide the entire group into two sections, and have them compete to see which side would sing louder.

Thursday evening of the last week, parents were invited to attend a program presented by the teachers and students. This offered a view of the Bible school experience. Of course, singing was a featured part of the program. Parents were impressed with how well the children sang. Many expressed appreciation to Dad for inspiring their kids to participate so energetically.

The Bible school was a rousing success. Richard had agreed to lead the school for one year, so there was a need for someone else to assume his superintendent role. With the benefit of having worked with Richard, Dad agreed to lead the Bible school, carrying the responsibility for several years. A good number of community kids became regular participants, and children within the congregation eagerly looked forward to Vacation Bible School as a highlight of their summer. Eventually, Dad turned over the administrative responsibilities to others, but continued to lead the singing for a few more years.

In retrospect, it seems apparent the Bible school outreach was a God-inspired directive. It helped the congregation recapture a fresh sense of mission. The initiative was also providential for Dad, providing a platform to impact the upcoming generation in a life-giving way. For years, Dad's passion for joy-filled singing and energetic music-making was imparted to the children of his congregation. Only eternity will reveal how profound that investment really was.

17

The Rich Routines of Home

The treasure of day-to-day living often escapes us. We easily treat the ordinary as mundane, failing to fully appreciate everyday occurrences. The passage of time can serve as a balancing factor. We are motivated to revisit and uncover the treasure of ordinary experiences taken for granted in those earlier days.

As children, there is much to savor and celebrate from our childhood years. We were blessed to live under the roof of Joe and Edith Clemmer. Our appreciation for the quality of their parenting has grown when viewed through the lens of an adult perspective. Today's pressures upon young parents are especially grueling. But the unique backdrop of the early 1940s produced its fair share of challenges for Dad and Mom as well.

As the impact of wartime began attacking the economic fabric of America, one consequence that significantly impacted Dad was gas rationing. At this time, he was farming in the daytime and giving music lessons several evenings each week. The imposed gasoline restriction was threatening to severely limit his teaching travels, and Dad was deeply troubled. It was painful to think of notifying students with the news he would no longer be giving lessons. The reduction in income would really hurt as well. There must be an alternative. If this calling to teach was valid, certainly the Lord could make a way. Sure enough, He did.

The Cushman scooter became the answer to Dad's prayer. With a rating of over sixty miles per gallon, this two-wheeled economy machine was just the ticket. Equipped with a side car for his guitar, Dad was back in business. After working on the family farm during the day, he would grab a bite to eat, fire up the Cushman, and be on his way. Rainy nights were a real test for Dad's perseverance. There must have been many times when he longed for the comforts of his '38 Buick. But the Cushman was making it possible for Dad to fulfill his passion to teach. Years of learning how to make sacrifices for higher causes served him well. In recounting those Cushman days, Dad would reference a sense of God's protection as, night after night, he weathered the elements.

The end of the war finally came. Gasoline restrictions became a distant memory recorded in annuals of World War II history. Shortly after the ending of fuel rationing, Dad made a visit to his car dealer friend, Herb Kuhn. Though his '38 Buick had been a good car, there were tell-tale signs it needed to be replaced. Dad got serious about purchasing a new Buick for his teaching travels.

With many of the automobile plants again reverting back to peace-time manufacturing, the fresh demand for cars had Detroit's assembly lines swamped. It was almost impossible to keep up with the demand for new vehicles. An order would take months to fill, with no clear word indicating how long the wait would actually be. Prospects for purchasing a new car were not looking good. Herb agreed to take Dad's order and do whatever possible to hurry it along.

A few weeks later, Herb called Dad. "Hey Joe, I just got a car in yesterday that was ordered by a fella in Souderton, and he decided not to take it. Would you be interested? This Buick has most of the extra equipment on it that you ordered. It's a four-door Super, but the color is maroon. I know you wanted black. What do you think?"

Dad was quiet for a few moments. Herb had said maroon, but Dad was thinking red. What would people say? Could he risk being misunderstood by many in the church who might view this as a major compromise? Herb was waiting. What should he say? "I'll take it," Dad answered. "I've got to go to the bank this afternoon and will stop by first thing tomorrow morning. Thanks for giving me first chance, Herb."

I'm not sure how Dad negotiated with Mom when breaking the news about deciding to buy the "red" car. Knowing Mom, she probably raised some of the same questions Dad had already been processing in his fast-working mind. But in the end, she agreed to submit to Dad's decision. Mom was committed to stand by her man when the kidding or criticism came. It did, and she did.

* * *

Though Dad was extremely busy with his work, he did enjoy indulging us in play. One favorite and unique activity we all remember from toddler years was "Drussa-Drussa-Drilly." Dad would bounce us up and down on his knee, reciting the Pennsylvania Dutch poem about a boy or girl riding a horse and falling off into the dirt. We would squeal with delight and beg him to do it over and over again. I [Janet] have enjoyed reenacting this action poem with my children and grandchildren. There's a good chance it will continue being rehearsed to future generations.

Often on Sunday evenings Dad played hide and seek with us. In the summertime we enjoyed playing baseball, croquet, and badminton in our spacious yard.

I'm grateful our parents taught us the joy of play, and also of work. We girls helped Mom wash and dry dishes, clean, and do other indoor jobs. She also taught us how to cook and bake, passing on many of our family's favorite recipes. The boys helped Dad with mowing the large lawn and other chores around the house. Dad had a creative eye for landscaping, so we had several beds of shrubs that required yearly edging, mulching and trimming. We all were enlisted for this project, and always heaved a great sigh of relief when that task was finally finished.

On rare occasions, Dad took us out to eat at a favorite restaurant he discovered in his music-teaching travels. Mom enjoyed these rare breaks from kitchen duty, and we children delighted in the novelty of eating out. One of those restaurants I remember was Ed's Diner in Doylestown. Another "eating out" highlight was stopping for soft ice cream, a new treat in the early '50s. I typically ate my cone very slowly so I'd have some to eat after everyone else was finished. The Frosty Cup on Route 309 near Souderton was one of the first in our area to offer soft ice cream. It quickly became a favorite hangout for young people.

* * *

Because of the high value placed on family and friend connections, sharing mealtimes with others provided a wealth of enjoyment for us. Family dinners at our grandparents' farms were memorable times because of the wonderful food and relational fun. These gatherings usually included uncles, aunts and cousins.

Grammy Alderfer's player piano was a major attraction. Each of us cousins would select a roll and wait in line until it was our turn to play. Pumping the pedals of that huge piano, we felt like accomplished pianists performing at a grand concert. When we went to Grammy Clemmer's place, a special treat was her delicious molasses nut candy that she stored in colorful tins. There were usually extra surprise treats as well.

Sunday evenings our family occasionally went to the Souderton Mennonite Home to visit Aunt Lizzie and Uncle Jacob. There was good reason for us children to endure the lengthy grown-up talk. At the appropriate time, Aunt Lizzie would signal us to follow her down the long hallway. Lizzie led us through the spacious kitchen to a large pantry. Rows and rows of large tin cans containing various food items lined the one wall. Lizzie chose a variety of cookies from the cans and put them in brown paper bags. Then she handed each of us our own bag of cookies. What a tasty reward!

Mealtimes at home were much more routine, but always appetizing because of Mom's great cooking abilities. Some favorite meals were fresh sweet corn, strawberry shortcake and Mom's beef pot roast with cooked carrots. Potato pie was at the top of our list. This was a Clemmer family recipe handed down through the generations, and we heartily embraced the continuation of that family tradition. Whenever Mom baked potato pie we made a meal of it.

Speaking of pies, all of the children inherited Dad's love for these delectable crusted desserts. Mom was especially skilled in the fine art of

The Cushman scooter, Dad's answer to the gas rationing crisis of World War II.

pie-baking. That may account for pie displacing the traditional cake at all our family birthday celebrations.

Homemade cookies were another specialty. Mom made lots of delicious cookies and stored them in the freezer in our basement. We were aware of this and often helped ourselves to a frozen cookie [or more] from this bountiful storehouse. The freezer was a great pit stop during our Saturday morning basement roller skating derbies. We attempted to rearrange the remaining cookies in those containers to make them appear untouched. Though Mom never let on, I believe she knew about us invading her cookie stash.

Dad and Mom were given to hospitality, opening their hearts and home to a multitude of people through the years. Mom, in her quiet way and with no fuss, could prepare a delicious meal for a number of people in record time. Dad was right there helping her. After the meat was carved, he would take off his apron and join the guests in the living room. At Mom's call, he would escort everyone to the dining room. There we would all enjoy a wonderful dinner and engaging conversation. Dad was a good entertainer and together he and Mom were an excellent team. They had a unique way of making their guests feel loved and treasured.

* * *

Dad gained a reputation for the pranks he played on friends during their visits to our home. One of his favorite tricks was the "plate lifter." I [Jan] remember setting our large dining room table and putting this gizmo under the tablecloth—an inflatable mini-balloon-type object strategically placed beneath a guest's plate. Thin tubing connected the balloon to a little rubber bulb under the table at Dad's place. This enabled him to inconspicuously squeeze air into the balloon at just the right time.

We decided who would be the recipient of the trick and made sure they sat at the designated place. In the midst of table conversation, Dad would squeeze the end of the cord which in turn caused that person's plate to move up and down. It was hilarious to see the funny reactions of the "victim" as they attempted to inconspicuously reposition their plate. Eventually the prank was exposed and everyone had a great laugh.

Dad also had fun with his dribble glass. It had a small disguised hole that leaked water when the person began drinking. The double suction cup between coffee cup and saucer was another favorite. Good fun mixed with good food made for a good time that all enjoyed.

A number of friends met the Fly Family when they visited. Again, Dad was the instigator. Each of us children stood in line, with a given name—Miss Butterfly, Miss Dragon Fly, Mr. Horse

Fly, and a few others. The guest was introduced, in turn, to each "fly." When finally encountering the last person named "Let Her Fly," that is exactly what happened—a hidden small glass filled with water unloaded on the unsuspecting visitor. We loved participating in that game, especially fulfilling the role of Let Her Fly!

Dad's humor was contagious. One cold evening in December when I [Jan] was twelve years old, Doris and I went outside to do a science experiment about the stars. Gazing intently into the star-studded sky, we were suddenly startled by a voice out of nowhere bellowing, "Hey you!" Startled, we quickly ran into the house and discovered that Wesley had secretly gone out the front door, taking great delight in the prospects of scaring his sisters. He was developing into a prankster just like his dad. Accustomed to humor and pranks, we naturally schemed to get him back.

Dad's humor was a wonderful gift to us during those growing-up years. Not only was our home atmosphere enriched, but we were also motivated to incorporate the value of humor when beginning our own families.

* * *

Christmas Eve caroling with our church friends was a yearly highlight. As children, we delighted in the prospects of a late night out. Dad was our enthusiastic song leader. Shivering in the cold December night, we gathered outside the homes of shut-ins and elderly church members to sing the well-known carols. Strains of "Joy to the World", "O Little Town of Bethlehem", and "Silent Night" wafted up into the cold night air. Ending with the rousing "We Wish You a Merry Christmas", we hustled to our cars and traveled on to the next house. At midnight the carolers returned to our house or Preston Allebach's place for a welcome smorgasbord of tasty cookies, steaming hot chocolate, delicious fudge, hot dogs, and the like.

In addition to scheduled seasonal happenings, there were occasional memory-making surprises. Sunday, February 16, 1957, the early morning snow began making roads treacherous. Royden and Erma Rittenhouse and Norm and Alice Rittenhouse, two of our aunts and uncles, were planning to come for dinner. They decided to come despite the weather and used a Jeep as their means of transportation. We all enjoyed Mom's home cooking and a light-hearted time of fellowship as the snow outside continued to accumulate. In a few hours they decided it was time to head for home through the drifted snow.

After our relatives left, we settled down for a long winter evening together as a family. Doris and I got supper ready while Dad started teaching Mom to play checkers. We brought supper into the living room on a cart and ate in front of the fireplace while the snow was blowing outside. Dad and Wesley later played checkers and some of us slept in front of the fireplace that night.

Monday, we were snowed in. It was quite different having the entire family at home on a weekday with no place to go. "Let's do something different for supper," Mom suggested. "We could make hamburgers over the fire." Lucy immediately caught the spirit of the moment and chimed in, "What about roasting marshmallows?" Everyone liked the idea of another meal around the fireplace. We spent the entire evening enjoying the warmth of the fire and the unique dimension of family togetherness orchestrated by God.

Tuesday we started shoveling the lane open. The road past our place still wasn't plowed. "I've never seen it this bad since we lived here," Dad remarked. By Wednesday the road was still impassable, lost in the landscape of huge imposing snowbanks. Dad decided to venture out, hoping to find a way to Harleysville. He actually was successful, traveling some of the way through open fields. Thursday we finally went back to school after experiencing an old-fashioned blizzard like those read about in storybooks.

* * *

We all attended Lower Salford School from grades one to eight. The school bus picked us up at the end of our lane. After a number of other stops, the bus finally arrived at the Vernfield General Store.

It then headed back down Route 63 finally arriving at the red brick school on Maple Avenue.

Memories of school days seem rather ordinary, but there were a few happenings that helped add a bit of special interest. The annual May Day celebration was spectacular to us. Lots of spring flowers were brought to the school grounds, helping to enhance the festive atmosphere. In the afternoon there was a large parade complete with floats, a marching band, a maypole dance, and several sporting events.

In the wintertime, ice skating was a popular sport. We were fortunate to have a sizable pond within walking distance of our house. When conditions were suitable, we spent many frigid evenings skating at the Alderfer pond. Those were fun-filled hours playing "crack the whip" and "stealing sticks" with only short breaks around the glowing bonfire to regain a bit of warmth. We also skated at our Uncle Norm's farm pond where Dad grew up, and on Godshall's Creek just a few miles from home. Godshall's was a popular skating place, especially Sunday afternoons. Dozens of families and couples joined us, often making me wonder if the ice was thick enough to support the crowd of skaters.

Christopher Dock Mennonite School opened on September 15, 1954, when I [Jan] was ready for ninth grade. It was the fourth Mennonite high school established in Pennsylvania, and the tenth in the United States. Our graduating class of thirty students was the first class to complete all four years at CD.

It was meaningful and interesting to have lessons taught with a Christian emphasis and to be challenged spiritually through chapel services. We also were given opportunities to use our talents in a variety of school activities and Christian service projects.

All-school and class socials were important events where we pulled taffy, enjoyed hay rides, played "Flying Dutchmen", "Reuben and Rachel", and other group games. For one social, I remember being asked to play an accordion duet with another student. At that time, musical instruments were not permitted on the premises, so we recorded our instruments and the tape was played at the event. It would not be until the 1964-65 school year that the musical policy was modified. Soon after this, the current senior class provided CDMS with an upright piano. This gift broke the ice. Future purchases of a nine-foot concert grand piano and an electronic pipe organ from Clemmer Music firmly established the acceptance of musical instruments into the arena of Mennonite education within the Franconia Conference.

* * *

Rich routines of home are occasionally seasoned with unplanned happenings that sometimes present themselves as negative intrusions. One of these came unannounced on a very hot and lazy summer afternoon. The heat and humidity seemed unusually oppressive. Gradually storm clouds gathered overhead and large drops of rain began dancing upon the parched lawn. Loud claps of thunder rumbled across the sky and bright bolts of lightning followed. Mom called all the children to the middle room. "I wonder where Dad is?" she questioned aloud, with a worried look on her face. "I hope he's with a student and not out on the road right now," she added apprehensively.

Suddenly, without warning, a huge bolt of lightning struck forcefully accompanied by an ear-piercing crack. Lucky, our dog, began barking incessantly. We huddled together, hoping it would soon end. Talking sporadically, we remained in the middle room till the storm passed by.

When it felt safe to venture outside, we took a look around. To our amazement, the top portion of our chimney had toppled over. There were bricks strewn over the roof and lawn below. Later while exploring upstairs, we discovered a few smoke-charred holes from the lightning bolt in the wall of Dad and Mom's bedroom. Fortunately, no one had been in the room at the time of the strike. After this incident Dad had lightning rods installed on our house.

Our dog, Lucky, was a vital part of daily family life for at least ten years. Lucky was a beautiful tan-colored collie. She was a gentle, playful dog. We sisters had fun dressing Lucky in doll clothes and teaching her to do various tricks. Wesley and Dean also took great pleasure in having Lucky as a partner in their play. When tenting in the back lawn, Lucky was always a part of their campout. She would position herself by the doorway, somehow sensing the need to assume a guard-dog posture for their protection.

Having such a personable pet was almost like having another sibling. One day Mom discovered dog hair on her toothbrush. After investigating, she discovered that two-year-old Dean had used it to brush Lucky!

As Lucky aged, we dreaded the day when she would leave us. Fortunately or unfortunately, we were spared the pain of a face-to-face good-by. Uncle Marvin, who lived next door, always fed and cared for Lucky whenever we took our family vacations. Upon returning home from a three-week family trip to California, he sadly informed us that Lucky had suddenly become lethargic and refused to eat. Though not being able to prove it, he figured she was saddened by our absence and had lost the will to live. We felt deeply grieved, all the while knowing her general physical condition was gradually deteriorating. It was a sad day. What a difficult experience it was adjusting to life without Lucky.

* * *

Daily routines provided golden opportunities for enriching parent-child interaction. I [Jan] remember having meaningful conversations with Mom while preparing meals or washing dishes. When I had problems and struggles Mom was very empathetic and understanding. Since she kept confidences, I felt free to share my heart with her. As I was growing up and had questions, she gave me wise answers. I knew I could count on her to be there for me. This gave me a sense of security, making home a shelter and refuge especially during those crucial teen years.

Mom and Dad were wonderful loving parents and provided priceless memories for us. The gift of loving family relationships and unique traditions has provided a valuable foundation for us to intentionally build upon. Since the death of our parents, we have established a new family tradition—an annual weekend sibling retreat with our spouses. In these gatherings, we continue to nurture the tradition of making more family memories. In our laughter, reminiscing, sharing and prayer, we strengthen the bonds developed with each other through the years. Life-giving family relationships are one of the greatest potential treasures worth nurturing.

18

On the Lawn

    A ringing of his desk phone broke the silence as Dad instinctively reached for the receiver. It had been an uneventful morning, catching up with some deskwork and paying a few bills. The call was actually a welcome diversion. Mom would soon be calling him for lunch.

    The voice on the other end of the line was a familiar one. Warren Moyer was not only Dad's minister at Towamencin, but also a personal friend. There was a strong mutual sense of respect between them. Warren genuinely appreciated Dad's energetic involvement as a Sunday School teacher, and was always affirming of his inspirational song leading.

    Warren's voice seemed a bit tentative as he spoke. "I finally got up with J.C. He told me to tell you to hold off for another year. He really didn't give a particular reason." Dad paused, mentally groping to sort out the full meaning of these words. He immediately felt a sense of anxiety and question tugging at his heart. What disappointing news! Obviously, Warren was just relaying the message. But somehow, it felt like both Warren and J.C. were not being very understanding of what seemed like a reasonable request. What could be wrong with moving the lawn concert to the high school location?

    Dad had high regard for Bishop J.C. Clemens. Several years earlier, when he and Mom had considered who should perform their marriage ceremony, there was little need for deliberation. It would be an honor to have J.C. officiate their wedding. He was highly respected in the larger Mennonite community, not just within the Franconia Conference. His reputation as an inspirational preacher was well known. J.C. communicated the Word in a way that brought freshness and life to the scriptures.

The bishop was also a very wise church statesman. Working through congregational issues with J.C. as a part of the process brought a seasoned dimension of wisdom to the table. He was open-minded and progressive, but never gullible. J.C. maintained a deep sense of passion to see the church move forward and had already contributed significantly to that cause.

And beyond all these strong points, Dad felt a special musical affinity with him. Not only was J.C. a gifted singer, but he also played the violin. J.C. had always seemed supportive of Dad and his involvement in music. That is what made this lack of consent even more puzzling. "Why can't J.C. and Warren hear my heart in this matter?" Dad mused to himself.

"Well, thanks for your efforts, Warren." Dad hung up the phone and pushed back his chair from the desk. What should he do? It seemed totally reasonable to move the recital location to Souderton High School. Yet, the bishop's response was a clear "no" spoken through a channel of authority he could not blatantly ignore.

Dad sat there, gazing out the middle-room office window. The view stretched across three large open fields to the home place. But for the moment, Dad was oblivious to the familiar landscape. Instead, his mind's eye drifted back in time, recalling the entire evolution of how these student recitals had been birthed. Momentarily, the heartache brought on by J.C.'s unfavorable verdict was swallowed up by heart-warming memories as Dad relived the play-by-play.

* * *

The vision for his concerts didn't really begin with Dad. The initial inspiration for these events was ignited in quite an unexpected way. It all started on a very ordinary day in the mid-1940s. Hiram Gross, one of Dad's buddies from church, had suggested the idea. "Joe, why

Approximately thirty-five students who traveled to Saylor's Lake in a multi-car caravan for a Sunday afternoon outing. These events were the forerunner of our annual sacred concerts.

don't you get some of your better students together and give a musical program on the lawn at our house? The parents of those students would come, and other friends as well. Mary and I would love to have you. How 'bout it?"

Dad was somewhat taken aback by Hiram's unsolicited invitation. Immediately his mind shifted into reminiscing mode. Dad recalled previous outings he had initiated with students in earlier years. They were real fun times. As many as twenty-five students would meet together on a Sunday afternoon and head for Saylor's Lake. It was a great social event, traveling together in a caravan of as many as a dozen cars. Dad even arranged for a motorcycle police escort to lead the lengthy motorcade on their hour-long excursion.

After arriving by the lake, trunks were unloaded, guitars tuned and accordions lugged from their cases. Then the group assembled to play their music. Other folks enjoying the delightful summer afternoon by the lake would saunter over and listen. Bystanders were curious to get a closer look at this unique musical band made up of young people playing familiar gospel songs with guitars and accordions. These were pleasurable events for the students, and very fulfilling for Dad.

But the musical happening Hiram proposed was different. How would it be accepted, gathering students together to present a program of instrumental sacred music right there on a lawn in the local community? The more Dad rolled the concept around in his mind, the better he felt about Hiram's idea. Giving students this opportunity to practice together and then present a formal recital for an audience could help develop their musical ability. It would also be enjoyable for the families. Practical details needed to be worked out, but the recital certainly seemed within the realm of possibility. "Let's do it," Dad responded, with a hint of growing excitement in his voice.

Dad embraced the recital vision and began to run with it. He eagerly contacted a group of his best students, and scheduled a few practice sessions. Enthusiasm began to build as the band of guitars and accordions took shape. Late that summer, the seed of Hiram's spontaneous suggestion became a tangible reality—an outdoor concert of sacred music on the lawn of Hiram and Mary Gross along the Forty-Foot Road near Lansdale.

It turned out to be a grand evening. A good number of friends, with blankets and chairs in hand, came to listen. Others who happened to drive by that evening parked alongside the road to take in this unique outdoor happening. Afterward, several of the students and friends bombarded Dad with their eager proposals. The verdict was unanimous. "What a great evening. You've got to do this again."

As Dad and Mom discussed the possibility of another recital, they felt one adjustment was necessary. It seemed better to move the event to their home rather than asking Hiram and Mary to host it again. Their large lawn next to the garage would make a great setting for the gathering. Another advantage was the empty field right below our house. It could serve as an ideal place for parking cars. A date was chosen and plans were finalized. Dad enlisted a few more students to participate in this repeat event. The annual Joe Clemmer Sacred Concert was born.

Word of mouth and news articles in the *Souderton Independent* brought an increase in attendance each successive year. Chairs were hauled in to provide adequate seating for the event. Volunteers were enlisted to help park cars. Programs were printed providing an order of service. In addition to songs played by the band, Dad included a variety of special solos, duets and trios performed by small ensembles of students.

The recital exposure immediately expanded Dad's reputation as an instrumental instructor. Inquiries for lessons mushroomed and Dad's teaching load increased rapidly. These concerts turned into a blessing far beyond his expectations. How amazing that Hiram's off-the-cuff idea would be the catalyst used to thrust Dad forward in fulfilling his music-pioneering call.

* * *

Though there was much to celebrate when considering the overwhelming success of these lawn concerts, some complications developed as well. Attendance at the recital had grown to about 200 people, and the supply of folding chairs available from the two churches was about exhausted. Parking was becoming a problem as well. Another concern was providing adequate rest room facilities. The two bathrooms in our house were being overrun. Mom had not anticipated this intrusion when agreeing to make her house accessible to those fifty or sixty friends and family members who attended the first year.

But the most crucial concern for scheduling an outdoor event was weather uncertainties. The year prior to Dad's appeal for the bishop's permission to relocate, the Saturday evening forecast had been quite threatening. There had been a lot of deliberating about whether to cancel the program. If a shower developed in the middle of the concert, it would cause a major disruption. Even a light drizzle could be due cause for concern, creating potential risk of damaging the musical instruments.

The father of accordion student, Nancy Sacks, told Dad later about spending most of that particular Saturday praying against the pending showers. It seemed apparent that God graciously intervened. Rain was reported all around the area, but somehow skipped over the Clemmer lawn. Dad was grateful for the favor of the Lord on that occasion, but it seemed unwise to contend with the possibility of a storm year after year. Because of the weather concern and the need for adequate parking, moving the recital to Souderton High School seemed like a great solution. But now, with J.C.'s refusal, what should he do?

Dad was not a rebel at heart. He wanted the blessing of his church leaders. Why could they not be supportive of his honorable intentions? Why did they not share his vision for encouraging young people to use their talents to honor God? What else could he do? This obstacle loomed before him as an insurmountable mountain.

It was unthinkable to cancel the recital. The students would really be disappointed. Should he go ahead and hold the concert one more year at the house? He could then simply make arrangements at the Souderton High next year without seeking permission from the church leaders. As Dad rolled this game plan over in his mind, it seemed like the only other possibility.

The sound of Mom's voice from the kitchen broke in to Dad's deliberating thoughts. "Joe, dinner's ready." As Dad headed from the office toward the kitchen, he felt a concerned reluctance about sharing the news of J.C.'s refusal with Mom. Yet he needed someone to help process the heaviness of his deep disappointment. Mom was a natural and caring listener. This was not the first impossibility they had confronted together. There must be an answer to this dilemma. Somehow, God would make a way.

19

Concert Expansion

Dad honored J.C.'s wishes, holding the concert on the lawn of our home for one more year. In 1951, without consulting Warren or J.C., Dad made arrangements to reserve the Souderton High School auditorium.

At the time, with seating for 1000 people, it was one of the largest public meeting facilities in the region. Other large community events were held at Souderton High. It had some of the more modern features of a large assembly hall—slanted floors, a huge stage, band pit and theatre style seating. This change in location was destined to increase visibility and accelerate the exposure of Dad's music to the entire region. A yearly reservation was locked in with SHS for the last Saturday of April, enabling interested folks to mark their calendars in advance and plan for the event.

People from other parts of the state began to hear about the recital and attend. This was especially true for the large Mennonite community in neighboring Lancaster County. Though somewhat more conservative than Franconia Mennonites, their love for hymns and gospel music attracted them to Dad's programs featuring instrumental arrangements of their favorite sacred songs.

As the word spread, a good number of Lancaster Mennonites made the yearly trip to Souderton High School to attend the recitals. In those days, attending an evening meeting that included round-trip travel of

150 miles was a significant excursion. With their more conservative dress, these Mennonites were easy to spot in the context of the local crowd.

Playing in the recital became a significant motivation for new students. Many children and teens who attended the Souderton concerts were inspired to begin taking lessons from Dad, primarily for the privilege of playing in the band. In addition to the fun of the concert experience itself, these budding musicians looked forward to those weekly rehearsals in preparation for the actual event.

Dad was a good leader. In our practice sessions, he had an outstanding ability to keep the players focused on the business at hand—pursuing excellence in making music. But Dad also scripted an atmosphere allowing these children and young adults to have a fun social experience as well. New friendships were formed around the common interest of making music. At the end of the April concert, many expressed disappointment in having to wait until February of next year for weekly practices to begin again.

* * *

As increasing numbers of students became eligible and excited about participating in the recital, Dad's vision was being reshaped and enlarged as well. The thrust of this concert ministry was taking him well beyond the initial vision of simply providing instruction for his students. It was also introducing his learners to a new kind of music-making experience.

Typically, recitals hosted by music teachers were focused on performance, showcasing talents of their up-and-coming students. However, this was not the case with Dad's recitals. Though there was a performance and showcasing element in the mix, something in addition to the obvious was at work.

It seems now, as I [Wes] take time to reflect back over Dad's musical journey, his sense of call to instruct was merely a spark to ignite a larger vision. Dad did not initially know God's intentions for his life's work, even when beginning to realize it was relating to music. His desire to teach students was merely a first-fruits expression of the larger calling and purpose prescribed for Dad.

This is often the way God works. As we begin to seek Him for direction, God introduces us to the first phase of our divine purpose. In an endless variety of ways, he inspires us to begin traveling that direction. We frequently start our purpose-pursuing journey with a significant degree of frustration. Straining to peer through the haze of the future, we strive to identify our ultimate destination—to know the will of God for our life. It seems relatively few find the will of God in a single moment of euphoric revelation. For most of us, the will of God unfolds as we proceed, step by step, in groping, obedient faith. Each step is a valid part of finding and fulfilling that purpose.

Through the progressive steps of Dad's musical pursuits, each forward step brought greater clarity regarding the fuller extent of his call. It was in the recital step that Dad began to discover a dimension of partnership with God more fulfilling than he had previously known.

God had clearly partnered with Dad in the initial step of learning the guitar. He was also definitely involved as a major partner in helping Dad become established as a teacher. It was divine inspiration prompting him to train and motivate individuals to honor the Lord through their music. But this recital step was somehow different. Calling together these individual students, providing them with the opportunity to harmonize their musical talents with others through the medium of sacred music—somewhere, without being consciously aware of it, a line had been crossed. The recital was becoming more than students playing notes and hymn tunes for the enjoyment of family and friends.

In reality, the musical happening was taking on the form of a ministry concert—an expression of praise and worship that provided actual ministry to the hearts and lives of people. Through the unique instrumental expression of these anointed hymns and gospel songs, listeners were actually being impacted spiritually. Attenders, some moved to tears, would frequently share testimonies of this ministry reality with Dad.

He had certainly intended to honor God with his music. Choosing to teach sacred music rather than promoting popular tunes of the day reflected this value. I doubt that Dad envisioned how the concerts would be used by God to attract and inspire thousands of people, even non-Christians. All of this was happening through a band of unprofessional musicians conducted by a leader who lacked formal musical training.

These natural deficiencies are similar to those reflected in the biblical story of the boy with his lunch of five loaves and two fishes. Though presented to Jesus in good faith, the food was totally insufficient to feed the multitude gathered to hear Jesus that day. Remaining in the hands of the boy, 5 + 2 = 7. But Jesus took those few natural elements, blessed them, and made much out of the little. In the hands of Jesus, 5 + 2 = 5000 with a remainder of 12. The insignificant lunch became a meal that fed 5,000 people with twelve baskets of food left over.

The lesson is obvious. We easily let math get in the way. In our hands, our gifts and talents don't add up, so we hesitate to offer them. But, when we give God everything we've got, there's no telling what He can do. With our little, He might use it to impact thousands of people just as He did for the young lad! This is exactly what happened with Dad's concerts. The "little" of teacher and students was being converted into much, much more.

20

Providential Partners

Providence—not an often-used word in our family during those growing up years. I'm sure Mom and Dad believed in the concept during that era, but didn't make much reference to it. But somewhere in Mom's journey, her awareness of God's providence was keenly quickened. What tuned Mom in to it? Her preoccupation may have been triggered through reading an inspirational article or possibly hearing a sermon addressing the subject. But I rather think her attentiveness to God's sovereign hand emerged in the course of everyday living.

Experience can be a profound teacher. Being married to a pioneer thrust Mom into a lifestyle she would have never chosen herself—living on the edge. More and more, with circumstances beyond her control, Mom needed to see the God who is in control. And she did.

Though naturally quiet, Mom could be a very powerful preacher. In later years, providence became one of her favorite, compelling messages. Over and over again, when an unexpected blessing or marvel surfaced right in the middle of everyday living, she'd exclaim, "That was providential!" Dear Mom discovered delight in giving credit to God who was working behind the scenes. It was a joy for her to observe people she loved being resourced and favored beyond their personal abilities and expectations.

Mom's eye for providence has rubbed off on me [Wes]. Inspired by her influence, I now find it fascinating to examine the threads of providence woven through Dad's life. I view those multi-colored strands clearly evidenced in men sovereignly ordained by God to intersect Dad's path. These providential partners each made their unique contribution in urging Dad forward to pursue his musical pioneering destiny. This partnering was especially crucial in times when Dad might have been tempted to shrink back.

* * *

Guy Heavener was a big man. He walked into our lives when I was a boy, and to me he seemed huge. When I first laid eyes on him, Guy kinda resembled the Goliath I imagined from the Bible story. A fascinating part about Guy's size was how he started out. Born premature, he weighed in at a bit less than four pounds. In those days, without the medical technology of our 21st century, Guy's survival was truly miraculous. As the story goes, his first couple of days fighting for life in the mountains of West Virginia were spent in a shoe box!

I forget the part of Guy's story that brought him north to the southeastern hills of Pennsylvania. By the time he entered the Clemmer story, Guy had become a highly visible and successful businessman in the region. His thriving coal, fuel oil and building supply company was based in downtown Harleysville. He also had a sizable fleet of Autocar trucks that hauled sand and stone into our area from out of state.

Guy was a man's man. His size and success made him seem invincible and somewhat intimidating. But underneath this tough persona oozed a tenderness that seemed uncharacteristic. At unannounced times this softhearted sensitivity would rush to the surface. These occasions seemed to be prompted by an inner spiritual stirring. Tears were the external manifestation. To see "Big Guy" weep was a wonder. This unique combination of toughness and tenderness was intriguing to me, and strangely attractive.

While immersed in his world of business, Guy was equally at home in things of the Spirit. A visionary in both arenas, he possessed a keen eye for hidden potential and innovative possibilities. So it's not surprising that his friendship was ordained as a providential setup, positioning him to assist Dad in his music pioneering ventures.

Guy had a missionary heart, with a special love for down-and-outers. He developed a connection with the Bowery Mission, an inner-city ministry immersed in the slums of New York City. During that era, Ray Allen served as director of the mission.

Ray had at one time been a respectable middle-class citizen with a wife and family. Through an unfortunate chain of events, he became a full-blown alcoholic, living as an outcast on the streets of New York. One night, desperately hungry and hopeless, Ray wandered in to the Bowery during an evening church service. The evangelistic gospel message hit its mark, and he was gloriously born again.

Though not able to reclaim his family and former status of life, Ray vowed to invest the remainder of his life helping others. He became absorbed in serving those on the streets who were still caught, as he had been, in the death-vice of desolation and drunkenness. His eventual role as superintendent of the Bowery was a perfect fit. Ray had been there, on the gutter side. He knew the unique struggles of these down-and-out men and could communicate the gospel in terms that powerfully penetrated their hardened hearts.

Guy loved visiting the Bowery. His heart was deeply moved by the needs of these men. He also connected instantly with the pastoral heart of Brother Ray. It was against this backdrop that Guy threw out his appeal to Dad. It likely popped up over coffee at Barbs & Babs, the local hometown restaurant that was just a stones-throw from Guy's building supply office. "Joe, how 'bout getting some of your students together and traveling with me to give a program at the Bowery Mission in New York?" After some further dialog, the end result was a group of Dad's students with their instruments headed for an encounter with the downtrodden of New York City.

What a culture shock! The tramps of our eastern Pennsylvania countryside looked well-heeled in comparison to these derelicts. It was one thing to hear second-hand accounts of beggars aimlessly wandering the sidewalks. It was quite another to observe block after block of these tattered Bowery outcasts.

Brother Ray welcomed our band warmly and immediately put us to work. His strategy was to have a few musicians stand on the entrance stoop of the mission and play familiar gospel songs. Immediately a group of street people would gather around to listen. Many of these had at one time been churchgoers, so they were acquainted with hymns like "Amazing Grace", "What a Friend We Have in Jesus", "Love Lifted Me" and "The Old Rugged Cross". Hearing again the familiar melodies of these songs stirred up feelings and reawakened memories of a long-forgotten God. After several minutes of this interplay, one of Ray's assistants would announce the evening service, inviting listeners to come and hear more. It was known that those who attended were entitled to a meal at the end of the meeting. Both physical and spiritual hunger wooed them in to the service.

That night, after numbers of men had filed in and taken their places on the darkly-stained pews, Brother Ray opened the service with a greeting and prayer. He then introduced Dad, and our band began to play. The hard-surfaced floors and walls along with the high ceilings of that old church sanctuary added reverb and volume, greatly enhancing our sound.

Some of the crowd seemed unmoved by Dad's music, but several began visibly responding to it. They started mouthing the words or singing along. These brain-numbed tramps were instantly recalling lines of lyrics almost forgotten from early boyhood years in church. Tender tears began trickling down their cheeks. The fallow ground of hardened hearts, calloused over by years of running from God, was being forcefully plowed up by these age-old gospel tunes. This was fitting preparation for the Word to be sown through the anointed preaching of Brother Ray.

During the altar-call that followed, it was quite moving to see several men head down the aisle to receive ministry and make their peace with God. Afterward, sharing a meal with these hungry and hurting men in the soup kitchen was a fitting climax to a very unusual but fulfilling ministry encounter. Heading back home later that night, there was much to reflect upon for both Dad and his band members. Everyone agreed enthusiastically, "Let's go to the Bowery again!"

This new door of music ministry Guy opened for the Clemmer band was highly significant. Playing our familiar gospel music in the inner-city environment of spiritual darkness was again extending Dad's music-making influence to a larger audience. However, there was something even more significant taking place within Dad himself—a new sense of mission. This experience of seeing the profound effects of

Providential Partners

Hagey's bus and the group of music students and friends who traveled to the Bowery Mission in New York City. Ellis Mack, pastor of Towamencin Mennonite Church, is on the far right.

sacred music deeply impacting broken people ignited a new fire within his pioneering heart. Previously, Dad had felt satisfaction in exercising his gift within the religious context of his home community. Now, experiencing the evangelistic dimension of his music and observing how it could be used by the Spirit to penetrate the needy hearts of derelicts—this was deeply fulfilling ministry and worth pursuing.

Many more Bowery trips followed during the next twelve to fifteen years. An increasing number of friends and family members became a part of our inner-city ministry excursions. Eventually it required two Hagey's buses to provide the needed transportation for these musical outreaches to the streets of New York City.

* * *

Another influencer and providential partner that crossed Dad's path in the mid-1950s was Walter Haman. Before his move to Harleysville, Walter spent several years of notoriety with the United States

Secret Service. One of his most colorful roles with the White House detail was serving as a bodyguard to President Roosevelt. During Walter's term as a member of FDR's entourage, he traveled extensively throughout many nations of the world.

This broad world exposure to the vast masses of hurting, needy people gripped Walter's heart. As this burden continued to grow, his concern gravitated to troubled youth. Walter felt if he could connect with struggling teens and challenge them regarding the costly consequences of sin, the Lord would honor his efforts.

Responding to this passionate sense of call, Walter terminated his Secret Service employment. His history as a presidential bodyguard was intriguing to people, giving Walter a huge amount of favor. With a law enforcement background, doors of opportunity opened that typically would have remained closed. He began traveling as an itinerant minister to young people, circulating among schools and juvenile detention centers with a dynamic message of challenge and hope. Though fulfilled in this evangelistic venture, Walter realized troubled youth need more than a motivational message to turn their lives around. A new beginning in a new place to begin a new life, was also required.

Walter began to envision establishing this kind of place—a Christian-oriented rehab center with resources to effectively restore troubled boys. In exploring possible properties for the venture, a good-sized farm for sale near Harleysville came to Walter's attention. Through a series of steps, he was able to purchase the property along Freeman School Road, and New Life Boys Ranch was born.

As a new Harleysville resident, Walter's connection with Dad came about quite naturally. One of his hobbies was playing the accordion. It was only a short time after moving to Harleysville that Walter heard about Joe Clemmer, the accordion man. He began taking music lessons from Dad, and those weekly interactions quickly became more than interchanges between teacher and student. As budding friends, they began interacting in a visionary sense as well.

Dad deeply respected Walter and his radical pioneering investment to help troubled teens find their purpose in life. It resonated strongly with his own passion to motivate young people to use their musical talents for godly purposes.

As the Boys Ranch became established, Walter continued working to build awareness and support for New Life, especially among the local community. Some of the townsfolk were naturally tentative about Haman and his ranch. Delinquent boys invading the local school felt somewhat threatening. Seeing these juveniles circulating downtown wasn't a welcome prospect either. New Life did host open-houses to familiarize local people with their vision, hoping to build trust. But these orientation events didn't provide sufficient opportunity to build ongoing rapport with the community. Something else was needed to fortify that connection.

It was out of this need that Walter's idea for Gospel Melody Roundups was conceived. His plan was to host regular music concerts in the meadow located near the large farmhouse. A Sunday afternoon of free inspirational entertainment provided by gospel music groups would likely attract a crowd from the local Christian community. Neighbors and people from the area coming to New Life for these events could connect relationally to the ministry. These happenings would also provide a built-in opportunity for sharing updates and to continue promoting the New Life vision.

Dad willingly agreed to help Walter launch these summer outdoor Melody Roundups. There were two or three programs scheduled during the course of each summer season. An open stage area with roof was constructed as a platform for the musicians. Attendees bringing their lawn chairs made it easy to accommodate whatever size crowd showed up.

The Roundup usually offered diverse styles of gospel music, attracting an assorted cross-section of listeners. At the invitation of Haman, four or five groups participated on a given Sunday, each one providing approximately forty minutes of music. Because of Dad's friendship and also our close geographical proximity, the Clemmer band became regular participants. Hugh Clinton's country gospel group was often there as well. At the time, Hugh was a singer who worked as a radio station announcer and disc jockey for WBUX Radio in Doylestown. Like many country gospel groups of the day, his Keystone Troubadours consisted primarily of family members. There were numerous other local and regional musicians who participated at those outdoor summer concerts. Some of Dad's students who went on to form their own groups played a part as well.

It is interesting to consider the providential impact these Melody Roundups had upon Dad's life. Though not drawing the large numbers of people that attended his yearly Souderton High concerts, these roundups provided a local endorsement of Dad's music by someone else from the local community other than himself. In Haman, a friend outside his Mennonite faith, Dad found a peer who valued his unique expression of instrumental music. And in God's providence, Walter also boldly initiated a creative idea to promote it.

I believe this meaningful partnership was a "divine compensation" for Dad. It helped him cope with the misunderstanding from church peers who could have opened doors of opportunity, but didn't. The roundups provided a setting for Dad to interact and relate regularly with other gospel groups in the area. He also welcomed this opportunity to renew acquaintances with old friends who had been long-time supporters and promoters of his music. One of the most notable of these promoters was Dave Hendricks—the Melody Roundup emcee.

* * *

Dave and Dad's paths had criss-crossed several times through the years. The first significant crossing of paths occurred in those weekly visits Dad made to the Hendricks home. As a young music lover, Dave had contacted Dad for guitar lessons. Though he didn't end up becoming a long-term student, those regular encounters provided ample opportunity for Dave and Dad to develop a special bonding through their shared passion for gospel music. Dave never seriously pursued his guitar playing, but did continue immersing himself in the music. After a few other jobs, Dave eventually landed a position as radio announcer and DJ at station WBUX in Doylestown.

Somewhat shy in personality, when Dave got behind a microphone in the studio, he was transformed into an enthusiastic and articulate communicator. People loved Dave's programs, and the station flourished because of his growing favor among the listening audience.

Though Dave enjoyed his work as a country music DJ, his first love was southern-style gospel music. Dave's dream was to someday own a radio station in his home area. The station would provide Christian programming, featuring a mix of gospel music and Bible-based ministry programs. That dream finally came to pass, and Radio Station WBYO in Boyertown became a reality. The timing was perfect, and this faith venture for Dave immediately became an astounding success. For years, the sizable Christian community had wished for a station that featured gospel music. The expanding listener audience supported WBYO whole-heartedly.

In the early days of the station, Dave wore many hats. One of those was selling radio spots to businessmen interested in advertising on his station. This brought another convergence of paths as he began interacting with Dad about designing advertising promotions for our flourishing music business.

One interesting side-note in this part of the Dave Hendricks story is worth mentioning. It was one of Dave's radio ads for Clemmer Music that caught the ear of a young Mennonite farmer in the Oley Valley of Berks County. Leonard Stoltzfus had been nurturing a keen interest for learning to play the accordion. Upon hearing the ad, Leonard immediately scribbled down the phone number. A few days later, he made contact with Dad and arranged for lessons. Little did Leonard know how providential that phone call would be. Not only did he take lessons and become proficient as an accordionist—he also got a wife. His eventual marriage to Doris, our oldest sister, made him the son-in-law of Joe Clemmer!

Through the years, Dave Hendricks and Dad had various occasions to partner together. Dave opened doors for Dad and his music in other states. At the grand opening of our music store, Dad enlisted Dave to do on-sight broadcasting from our new business location. Whenever the opportunity presented itself, Dad and Dave welcomed the chance to promote one another's ministries.

Providential partners are a tremendous gift. Dad was blessed to have several of these partners to walk and work with through the years. They not only believed in him as a person, but were willing to generously invest themselves to help Dad fulfill his pioneering pursuits.

21

Music-Man Merchandising

An attic is a handy place. It's great for storing the hodgepodge of seasonal clothing or out-dated "stuff" accumulating over years of living. We had a small sampling of this assortment in the small attic next to the dormer bedroom. But the majority of space was occupied by upright cardboard cartons. These boxes contained an interesting assortment of guitars and accordions.

In my early boyhood days, I [Wes] can remember Dad receiving a call from the railway office announcing the arrival of one or two instruments for pickup. As Dad and I headed for Souderton, I eagerly anticipated having an up-close look at those black-iron engines steaming in and out of the station. After returning home, Dad would inspect the new instruments making sure there was no hidden damage. Then we toted them upstairs to be stored in the attic stockroom.

It was a distinct disadvantage not having the visibility of a commercial store to attract off-the-street buyers. Offsetting this limitation was the built-in potential of Dad's loyal student clientele. This coupled with the low overhead arrangement of an in-home business allowed him to develop a respectable volume of retail sales.

As Dad's students advanced, he would recommend to the students' parents that they consider purchasing a better instrument for their budding musician. An appointment would be scheduled for them to come and check out Dad's attic inventory of new instruments. Mom's living room was instantly transformed into a music store showroom.

Before the buyers arrived, I helped Dad lug an assortment of instruments from the attic—four to six within the price range and quality suitable for the student. We would line them up in a row on the living room floor with case lids open, and the sales session would begin.

Dad went down the line, talking about the selling points of each model. A vital part of his sales pitch was with instrument in hand. As Dad played, he described the differences in sound and ease of playing. He knew his stuff, and it was usually only a short time until the delighted child was headed out our front door with a new instrument in hand. Dad and I celebrated the sale by carting the remaining instruments upstairs again, placing them in cartons until the next sales appointment. Though this unique merchandising arrangement worked well for a number of years, the events of a spring day in the late 50s was destined to radically change the future of our in-home business.

It was lunchtime, and the Gibson guitar salesmen, Orn Sepp, had just left. Dad strode out to the kitchen, exclaiming to Mom, "Guess what I just bought?" Mom looked up from her lunch preparation with an inquisitive smile. "What now?" she asked. "An organ!" Dad replied, with a gleam in his eye. Though Mom was somewhat accustomed to Dad's adventurous approach to life and work, this announcement caught her totally by surprise. "You'll never sell an organ!" she countered. Mom was normally a solid supporter of Dad, but this prospect was going beyond what she had faith to envision.

At the time, our living room was graced with one or two pianos. Though Dad did not teach piano, he had begun selling a few instruments to families of his guitar and accordion students. Mom had graciously given away some of her precious living room space to accommodate the expansion of Dad's business. Now, this prospect of an organ on display would require even more sacrifice from her. What an eventful day! Even Dad had no way of envisioning how significantly this new business initiative was to impact their future.

The Lowery organ finally arrived. As the tractor trailer pulled out of our driveway, Dad and I began the task of unpacking this fascinating keyboard instrument. It was an instant hit. Doris and Janet, with their accordion and piano background, began to immediately explore its novel sounds. Dad's enthusiasm for promoting the organ began

Dad leaving the house to begin an afternoon and evening of teaching guitar and accordion. This 1953 Super model was the last of his black Buicks.

rubbing off on his accordion students. It wasn't long before Clemmer's Musical Instrument Supply Co. was making its mark locally in the exploding home organ business.

Living room merchandising was being taken to a new level. The string of patrons frequenting our house now included not only guitar and accordion customers, but organ buyers as well. Fortunately for me, we didn't need to transport organs back and forth from the attic. But unfortunately for Mom, her living room was shrinking to make way for the expanding lineup of instruments available for sale.

Our large living room was a great asset to Mom in exercising her gift of hospitality. This invasion of her space must have been more difficult to resolve then she let on. But again as in so many other instances, Mom's servant heart won out. Making the best of this new limitation, she adjusted the size of her dinner guest lists and continued blessing friends with her wonderful hospitality gift.

The living room intrusion wasn't the only part of our home turf impacted by Dad's expanding music business. The front lawn was destined for invasion as well. All progressive retail businessmen would heartily agree. To do a good job of merchandising, you need a sign. This was a no-brainer for Dad. The organ salesman encouraged him as well. Dad's visionary mind had little difficulty coming up with a good sign idea. It needed to be large enough for easily visibility. Having a lighted sign at night would be an advantage as well. A majority of customers shopped in the evening hours. A brick base serving as a planter for flowers was incorporated in the design, making the sign more attractive.

Again, Mom was not very excited about the sign idea. She had no desire for her home to take on the likeness of a storefront. A large 5 ft. x 3 ft. fluorescent sign with "LOWREY ORGANS" inscribed on the glass panels—it definitely was not her idea of front lawn landscaping enhancement. But the writing was on the wall. Dad's business had turned a significant corner, now headed aggressively in a new direction. There would be no turning back.

Progress inevitably involves positives and negatives, and success in life requires knowing how to flow with both. Though Mom never developed the skills of an accomplished musician, she certainly acquired an unusual ability to harmonize. When her conservative preferences threatened to discord with Dad's progressive pursuits, she chose instead to harmonize with him. Peace at home was more important than having her way.

Launching into the organ business introduced yet another new ingredient into the mix. Closing a sale meant that a delivery needed to be made. Unlike guitar and accordion sales, organs could not be toted home on the rear seat of a customer's car. Initially, we borrowed a truck for organ deliveries, but this was highly impractical. We needed a delivery van.

During that era, the VW bug had become a very popular vehicle. It was compact, economical, and relatively inexpensive. The VW line of vehicles also included the VW mini-bus and a similar body style without windows—a mini panel truck. Dad did the research and found the VW truck would be an ideal vehicle for organ deliveries.

Being a devoted Buick man, Dad was breaking out of the mold big-time in considering the purchase of a VW. No dealers in our area sold these vehicles, so he traveled to a suburb of Philadelphia to check out VW vans. The salesman had an easy sell with Dad. There was no question. The mini panel truck was just the ticket for organ deliveries. Dad struck a deal, and the little blue van was added to our vehicle fleet.

At the time, Dad had two Buicks because of multiple drivers in the family. Doris also had her own Buick, so our three-car garage was full. There was some extra garage space with a walk-in door that housed our lawn mower and bikes. Dad's innovative mind went to work and came up with a plan. Though a tight fit, there was enough room to back the VW into that extra space. The mower and bikes could be grouped tightly together in front of the van. The Buick next to the van would require moving every time the van was needed, but that was workable. So, with our living room showcasing three to five organs, the attention-getting sign in the front lawn, and the VW van, we became fully immersed in the organ business.

22

Inspiration and Reproduction

As Dad continued immersing himself in his teaching profession, he enrolled students with a wide diversity of musical motivations and aspirations. Some adults who sought him out were chasing a left-over childhood dream. They signed up with Dad for fifty cents a lesson, hoping to learn an instrument for their own personal enjoyment. Their time with Dad was rather brief. Others were more serious. They fell in love with their instrument, enjoyed Dad's enthusiastic teaching, and became long-term students.

Children and youth always represented the larger percentage of his student list. They often were enrolled for lessons because of the musical priorities embraced by their parents. Traditionally, music-making was a value handed down through the generations. In Dad's early teaching days, parents still were tuned in to the multiple benefits available to children who studied a musical instrument—personal discipline, creative expression, character building, and the like. With this firmly held value of music-making, parents were motivated to make significant sacrifices to provide this enrichment opportunity for their children.

I [Wes] remember Dad sharing an intriguing bit of insight he gleaned from Orin Sepp, our Gibson guitar salesman. Orin represented the perfect picture of an upper society businessman. He was wealthy enough to periodically take multi-week sailing excursions on his own private yacht.

Two of Dad's young students representing literally hundreds who were introduced to the joys of music-making by him.

With an unusually keen eye for economic trends and a long history of music-merchandising, Dad often solicited Orin's seasoned perspective.

In one of those brainstorming discussions, Dad posed a very logical question. "What might happen to the music business in the event of a major economic downturn? It would seem logical to categorize music lessons and instrument purchases as a non-essential luxury. Wouldn't these expenditures be the first ones eliminated when families experienced financial reversal?"

Orin's observation was a surprise. He reported that, during the Great Depression, just the opposite was often true. In actuality, parents were willing to do without some other essentials "so that Johnny or Susie could continue their music lessons." In other words, parents were highly motivated to sacrifice something temporal in order to provide a life-long benefit for their child.

Dad's experience through his years of teaching confirmed this reality firsthand. Multitudes of parents sought him out, highly motivated to pay for quality musical instruction to enrich their child. Many purchased lessons for multiple children and continued doing so for years. These parents were willing to make substantial personal sacrifice, primarily because of envisioning the long-term payoff reaped by their offspring.

In addition to noble parental motivations, many children and teens who became Dad's students were self-motivated. In some providential way, a desire to play music had been sparked within them. These flames of inspiration were usually ignited by an influencer—a personal friend who played, or a well-known musician they admired. The young aspiring musician would then pester their dad or mom for an instrument and lessons. Time after time, a parent would come to Dad with the typical line, "My child keeps hounding me for a guitar and lessons, so I guess there will be no rest until we get them started."

Young, eager-beaver beginners were a delight to Dad. He loved to take boys and girls with a glimmer of interest and fan that spark into a flame of developed musical ability. Of the thousands he introduced to music-making, many never persevered beyond the elementary or intermediate stages of accomplishment. This in no way discounts the payoff to these low-level achievers. It is well documented that music-making represents tremendous value to the maker, even in its very simple and crude forms. Hundreds and hundreds of amateurs were introduced to the enjoyment of creating music on their instrument—all because Joe Clemmer sat on their couch, week after week, showing them how.

But sprinkled among the masses of this unprofessional majority were a few aspiring musicians destined to receive far more than musical "show-how" instruction from Dad. One of these musician "sons" who sat and gleaned at Dad's feet was Jack Bechtel.

* * *

Jack, later known as Big John, didn't start out as a complete novice with Dad. When Dad showed up at his door along Main Street in Telford, Jack had already begun whetting his musical appetite. This took place at the keyboard of a well-respected piano teacher on Hamlin Ave. From 1942 to 1946, Jack dabbled with piano under Mrs. Flouck's tutelage. But without sustained motivation, his interest disintegrated into thin air.

A bit later, Jack happened to come across Arthur Godfrey playing his baritone uke on TV. Something immediately sparked within Jack. He pulled the Sears Catalog off the shelf, ordered a ukulele, and began picking his way through simple tunes that Godfrey taught. With this flame of interest in string music flickering, the guitar music of country and western singers on TV began to grab his ear. Again, Jack thumbed through the Sears book, selecting a good-looking rhythm guitar from the line-up. He waited eagerly for the delivery of his new Harmony six-string instrument.

By this time, Wesley, Jack's dad, was awakening to the reality of his son's potential musical ability. He needed to find a local guitar teacher to help Jack on his way. There is a possibility Wesley went back to piano teacher, Mrs. Flouck, for a reference. Mildred Flouck and Dad were well acquainted. Not too long before, Dad had enlisted her to provide piano lessons for Doris and Janet. It was during this time of Wesley's search that Mildred was making weekly Saturday morning visits to the Clemmer house. She respected Dad, and would likely have recommended him to Wesley.

After only a few lessons with Jack, Dad made a rather unusual suggestion. He had no way of knowing how monumental his recommendation would be in altering the course of Jack's musical destiny. "Jack, since you really wanta play rhythm and not lead guitar, why don't I install a raised nut and show you how to play slide-guitar style rhythm?" Dad questioned. That sounded okay with Jack, so Dad made the conversion.

Some weeks later, observing how Jack was progressing on his adapted Hawaiian guitar, Dad offered a bit of counsel to Wesley. "Jack is really doing great with his instrument, and I would advise you to consider investing in a better one. I've got a new model Supro Hawaiian electric with matching amplifier at the house. It would be great for Jack. Why don't I bring it along for his lesson next week?" Wesley gave the okay, and that is how Jack was introduced to his first electric Hawaiian guitar. Now, with an instrument capable of creating the genuine "steel guitar" sound, Dad switched Jack over from simple chording and began teaching him from the Hawaiian music course.

Those elementary Hawaiian lessons that transpired in the following months probably seemed rather routine to both teacher and pupil. But in hindsight, it seems apparent something more than basic instruction was in the mix. Without Dad's conscious awareness, impartation was also taking place. It was as if the first love of the "father" was awakening the first love potential inherent in the "son."

Dad appreciated and enjoyed each of the instruments he taught, but Hawaiian guitar was his first love, hands down. The person who likely imparted that passion to Dad was Eddie Alkire. Though Dad was attracted to the Hawaiian guitar before they met, it was probably Eddie's fatherly inspiration and impartation that settled the first love contest for Dad's musical heart. And now, he was inspiring Jack in a similar way.

Though Eddie's impartation was primary, he was not the only "well" from which Dad drank. I can remember as a young boy, cutting my teeth of musical appreciation on Dad's assortment of 78 RPM records. Though his collection was not large in number, four names made up the majority of his albums. Eddie Arnold and Red Foley were two of his singing entertainer preferences, but Sol Hoopi and Jerry Byrd were his favorite steel guitar inspirations.

* * *

Solomon Hoopi Kaaiai was born in 1902 in Honolulu, Hawaii, the youngest of twenty-one children. He began playing ukulele at age three, and soon added guitar and Hawaiian guitar to his music-making pursuits. In 1919, following the lure of his wanderlust spirit, Sol stowed away on an ocean liner and ended up in San Francisco. From there he made his way to Los Angeles, and continued pursuing his musical career on the mainland.

Sol's first recordings in 1927 featured acoustic slide guitar. With the evolution of guitar amplification, he switched to electric lap steel around 1935. At the same time Sol began experimenting with different tunings. Minor key tunings allowed for more sophisticated chord and melody work than the standard tuning in use at the time. In the spirit of a pioneer, Sol became renowned for his blues-influenced sound. He applied it to the standard songs of the day as well as to old Hawaiian favorites. Hoopi's great notoriety and success in the music field also opened other doors for performing in movies and entertainment shows.

As 1938 approached, no one guessed what significant changes that year held for Sol and his illustrious career. Prompted by a personal spiritual encounter, Sol Hoopi began making major course corrections for his musical future. With the turn of his heart, Sol began including sacred music in his extensive repertoire. He also joined the crusade of evangelist Aimee Semple McPherson.

Hoopi was likely one of Dad's greatest musical heroes. He was inspired by Sol's tremendous musical expertise and pioneering creativity on the steel. But I believe Dad was especially drawn to Sol because of their shared love for sacred music. Those were the records Dad treasured most – Sol playing the hymns he loved, Hawaiian style.

* * *

Dad's other favorite steel guitarist was Jerry Byrd. Though Byrd was strongly influenced by traditional Hawaiian music, he made his legendary impact outside that arena. Jerry is credited as one of the primary forerunners to integrate the sound of steel guitar into country and western music. In the early 1950's Jerry entered the doorway of notoriety during his stint in the band of country singer, Red Foley.

It is widely affirmed that Jerry Byrd has been a greater inspiration to budding steel players than any other musician. Jerry is also recognized as the one most responsible for defining the early

Nashville steel guitar sound with his trademark vibrato and lush C6th tuning.

Little wonder that Dad's attraction to Jerry Byrd also became an attraction for his guitar student, Jack. Though Dad enjoyed listening to Jerry, he didn't have the time needed to explore the intricacies of Jerry's unique style. The demands of family and church responsibilities along with his flourishing teaching career would not afford Dad that luxury.

This was not true for Jack. As a young adult, he had the two necessary commodities—time and motivation. Jack scanned the radio dial for shows featuring country music that included airplay of Jerry Byrd's record releases. With his keen musical ear, Jack realized the tuning Jerry played was different than the A tuning used by Dad. He was wowed by the more complex sounds of Jerry's C6th tuning, and wanted to explore its possibilities.

Attempting to honor both his respect for Dad as well as his passion to learn Jerry's tuning, Jack did an amazing thing. Every week, between lessons with Dad, he would remove the six strings on his Supro. Jack would then restring the guitar with the appropriate gauge used by Byrd and retune to C6th. Then, just before his lesson, he would convert back to Dad's tuning to take his lesson. This went on for quite some time, without Dad's knowledge.

Jack's capability to keep advancing on both these fronts is a testimony to the unusual talent and outstanding motivation he possessed. Though Dad did not know the extent of Jack's guitar explorations, he certainly recognized Jack's innovative bent. As a true father, he went out of his way to fuel the fire in his musical son. Therefore, when Eddie Alkire began introducing Dad to his 10-string Hawaiian guitar invention, it was a natural for Dad to also introduce Jack to this new pursuit. It wasn't long before Jack made his pilgrimage to Easton with Dad to meet Eddie. The outcome was inevitable—Jack bought an Eharp and began exploring the intriguing chromatic tuning. In so doing, he added yet another breed of steel guitar picking to his weekly practice routine.

Fully aflame in his music pursuits, Jack also began taking accordion lessons from Dad. A bit later, he again picked up the study of regular rhythm guitar on his own. Part of this renewed inspiration to play guitar was from watching "The Tennessee Plowboy," Eddy Arnold, on TV. This is especially noteworthy, since Eddie Arnold was also a primary inspiration to Dad.

It was during these years of pouring into Jack that Dad was becoming solidly established and recognized in the region as a highly sought-after instrumental instructor. With the constant stream of inquiries for lessons, Dad was scrambling, trying to rework his schedule to allow for more half-hour slots.

* * *

The count of students now began inching past the 100 mark. In addition, he had a waiting list of others interested in signing up. This was an exhausting pace. Not only did Dad's time investment involve the actual teaching session for each student, but also the travel time from house to house.

To teach 100 students weekly, Dad would generally leave the house between 6:30 and 7:00 each weekday morning. This allowed him to give two or three lessons before taking the last student to school. Each afternoon, Dad picked up his first student at school, and drove them home for their lesson appointment. The rest of the afternoon and evening was scheduled tightly until 9:30 or 10:00 at night. Monday through Friday was essentially a repeat of that same grueling routine. Saturday was another full day of teaching from early morning until late afternoon. Though greatly fulfilled in his work, Dad was at the brink of exceeding his limits. There was no way he could sustain this pace indefinitely.

Dad's dilemma did ultimately have a positive outcome. The reasonable solution dawned one day as Dad was again revisiting his schedule dilemma. Suddenly it hit him! Why not begin giving some of his beginner guitar students to Jack? He was by now quite accomplished, and certainly capable of learning to teach. Jack was willing to try his hand at teaching, so Dad began assigning students from his waiting list to Jack. This plan not only provided immediate help to relieve Dad's overloaded schedule, but it also introduced him to the great leadership principle of impartation and reproduction. What a joy to discover the fulfillment of extending his influence by multiplying himself through others.

During this season of partnership, Dad invited Jack to join him on a trip to Chicago. Together they traveled to attend the National Association of Musical Merchants convention. All the big-name instrument manufacturers gathered at this trade show to promote their new products. The yearly event provided hundreds of dealers like Dad with the advantage of one-stop shopping—buying from manufacturers all over the world. It also was an ideal opportunity to build relationships with new suppliers.

Jack was in his glory. This was almost heaven, having the opportunity to see and try out guitars he had previously only dreamed about. Dad was delighted to see Jack having such a good time. The music convention trip added another layer of richness to their already meaningful working relationship.

Though Jack was successful as a teacher and enjoyed working with Dad, his first love was performance. Having progressed from lap steel to pedal steel, Jack began seeking out jobs with the bands of local entertainers. Establishing himself within this circle of regional performers began introducing Jack to an even larger network of professional musicians. Doors continued to open. Moving on to the Wheeling Jamboree in West Virginia, Jack eventually made his debut at The Grand Ole Opry in Nashville.

Eventually, Jack and his wife made the decision to move to Tennessee. There his reputation as a pedal steel innovator and top-notch musician continued to grow. Having gained the attention of nationally known entertainers, Jack was hired and did extensive tours with big-name singers throughout the nation and abroad.

Dad hated to lose Jack, but he felt honored, knowing his fathering investment of inspiration and impartation had helped Jack become an accomplished professional guitarist. Though their working relationship was terminated, the friendship continued. Often, Jack would stop by the store during periodic visits with his parents. These interchanges were always a treat for Dad. Both he and Jack savored the chance to reminisce, fondly reliving the good times they experienced together. These visits also included another important dynamic. They became an occasion for Jack to interact with my brother, Dean, in his early pedal-steel pursuits. While respecting Dad's lap steel influence, Dean was reaching for the innovative sounds of the next generation. Fortunately, Jack was available to provide that inspiration.

Jack was only one of several who not only received inspiration and impartation from Dad, but were raised up by him to teach others. Yes, it was a joy for Dad to discover the fulfillment of extending his influence by multiplying himself through other influencers. As one of his blood sons, I [Wes] feel especially blessed by his inspiration and reproduction influence. Consequentially, passing on what has been imparted to me has become a primary motivation of my life. After all, reproduction is the key ingredient in fulfilling family destiny. It's the essence of a living legacy!

23

Note-Worthy Trips

As has been mentioned before, the Bowery Mission encounter was a life-changing event for Dad. Prior to that experience, his music had been presented to and received by his own people—rural, conservative middle-class America. Dad knew his audience and well understood how to reach them through the medium of uplifting gospel music.

In stark contrast, at the Bowery, he suddenly found himself worlds away, thrust into the heart of a diverse inner-city culture. Here he was, ministering to down-and-outers. This people group was extremely difficult to reach. And yet, the Spirit of God had anointed his unique style of music to break open hard hearts and change lives. This experience was profound. It ignited a new desire within Dad to impact more people in other places. His visionary pioneering spirit shifted into overdrive.

If taking his music on the road was to be a more regular occurrence, it seemed right for Dad to hand-pick some of his better students and form a traveling band. With very little deliberation, he chose to name our band "The Musical Messengers." This group usually consisted of ten to twelve players, the maximum number that could conveniently travel in two cars.

Even as Guy Heavener had been the initial door-opener for Dad's Bowery Mission contact, he continued this role in promoting The Musical Messengers. With roots in West Virginia, Guy went to work contacting pastors and community leaders in his hometown region. The first of these music ministry trips took place in the mid-1950s.

Snaking our way down the endless switchbacks of those remote West Virginia mountains was a novel experience for us. Our destination was Hetrick's Motel, owned by one of Guy's blood relatives. We unloaded our luggage and grabbed a bite to eat at the restaurant across the road. Traveling south a few miles, we arrived at the small-town high school where our Saturday evening concert was scheduled. These folks had never heard of The Musical Messengers. Even so, a good crowd showed up and seemed to really enjoy our music.

Though the focus of this trip was ministry, we eagerly took advantage of free time between concerts to do some sightseeing. Guy was delighted to serve as our tour guide, escorting us to the most popular scenic attractions. Some of these places etched in our memory include the spectacular panoramic views from Spruce Knob, the torrents of water rushing over Black Water Falls, and the huge, unusual rock formation named The Mouth of Seneca. After completing our final program for the weekend, we returned home with a sense of great fulfillment. Savoring the memories, we longed to make a return trip to West Virginia. And we did.

* * *

Future trips in the latter 1950s and early 1960s also took us to a neighboring West Virginia community in the southern region of the Canaan Valley. Years earlier, Sam and Margaret Bucher had left their home in eastern Pennsylvania to pioneer a medical mission work in the heart of Appalachia. They settled on a piece of property along Route 32, near Harman, West Virginia. There Doc Bucher carved out a mountain clinic complete with examination rooms, a small infirmary, and personal living quarters.

Sam and Margaret were good friends of Dad and Mom. Hearing that Dad was traveling with his musical group, they extended an invitation, booked our program itinerary, and rolled out the red carpet for us. Guy and Alice Heavener also knew the Buchers and were delighted to offer their big Chrysler and head south with us.

These West Virginia weekends were a delight in multiple ways. The girls slept in hospital beds at the clinic and in a guest house near the edge of the property. Many wonderful memories were made in this cozy cabin by the warmth of the fireplace and in the loft where they slept. A bubbling mountain brook flowed by the cabin providing a relaxing serenade, lulling them to sleep. For the guys, their accommodations were a bit more rustic—a converted chicken house at one of the neighbors. This setting provided a more authentic dose of genuine mountain life.

One of the highlights on these excursions was the spontaneous chemistry of humor triggered between Sam, Guy and Dad. They egged each other on, creating a hilarious marathon of laughter, pranks, and jokes. Everyone was drawn in to their antics. This liberal dose of good-natured fun quickly made us feel like one big happy family.

Coupling relational fun with ministry was formative for us. It was valuable to discover first-hand how serving others could at the same time be pleasurable. We also learned that a key ingredient to ministry fulfillment is the intimate relationships formed in the context of the work.

On the first of these Harman trips, our initial musical event was a concert at the Harman High School. We were amazed to see the auditorium fill up with mountain people eager to hear our music. Sunday morning we gathered our instruments and headed for High Rock Church just a few miles from Harman. This congregation met in a picturesque little white building along a narrow dirt road near the top of a mountain. After the service, we went to the home of a church family for an outdoor picnic. They treated us to a great feast of southern home cooking that hit the spot.

During future trips to West Virginia, we occasionally had spontaneous spur-of-the-moment assignments added to our itinerary. On one of those unscheduled Saturday afternoons, Doc Bucher asked Dad if our group would like to visit two blind sisters—friends who lived in a home tucked way back in the hills. Unable to attend any of our programs, they would feel honored by a personal visit. Both women loved to sing the hymns of the church. Doc knew our music would be a great encouragement to them.

Dad's Buick and Guy's Chrysler wound through the mountains until we came to a run-down shack standing by itself in the corner

*Taking our music to the mountains of West Virginia.
Our mission in this photo is bringing cheer to the home of two blind sisters.*

of a secluded, hillside meadow. After parking our cars alongside the dirt road, we lugged a few accordions and a couple of acoustic guitars through the sloping field to their simple dwelling. Upon entering through the crooked outer door, we stepped into the main room, dimly lit by a small table lamp. A bit of outside light filtered through the few small windows. As our eyes gradually adjusted to the darkened living area, it was fascinating to spot a calendar from the 1940s with President Roosevelt's picture on it. Looking across to the other side of the small room, we were taken aback to see gaping cracks in the outside wall. I [Jan] almost shivered, imagining how cold that room would be in the dead of winter.

After the guitars were tuned, we began playing and singing old gospel favorites like "Blessed Assurance", "Great Is Thy Faithfulness", and "In the Garden". Immediately these two sisters began singing with us. It was inspirational to observe their heart-felt exuberance as we praised the Lord together. Both faces reflected a radiant heaven-like glow. Blinded to earthly surroundings, their spiritual sight seemed unusually keen in beholding heavenly realities.

As I looked around and observed how little they possessed of this world's wealth, I was deeply inspired by their overflowing happiness and contentment. They had obviously discovered the secret of living joyously in spite of great lack.

We had come, thinking the primary agenda was for us to brighten their day. After our good-bys, we left with the profound sense God's greater intent may have been for these blind ladies to inspire and enlighten us. It was a very moving experience I've never forgotten.

* * *

A few other Musical Messenger excursions in that era were arranged by Dad's good friend, Dave Henricks. Though Dave's career in radio began locally, he later pursued broadcasting opportunities out of state. One assignment was as a program director and disc jockey at a station in Staunton, Virginia. With a strong passion for promoting gospel music, Dave contacted Dad about bringing his band to Staunton for a weekend of programs. As a part of our itinerary, Dave included an unexpected extra—a half-hour studio session playing "over the air." That was quite a switch, performing in a small broadcast studio, but all the while being heard by a large, unseen audience. Upon hearing about the studio session, we were all eager to experience what it was like "playing on the radio." Afterward, everyone agreed playing for a live audience was much more fulfilling. We preferred an interactive audience.

A year or two later, Dave moved from Staunton and took another broadcasting position at a Christian station in Cheraw, South Carolina. Again, he contacted Dad to line up a similar weekend of programs in this new location. It was great to have Guy Heavener join us for this weekend of meetings.

Because our last program was a Sunday evening church service, we planned to drive a few hours and then stop at a motel before finishing our trip the next day. Heading north on Route 301 between Fayetteville and Rocky Mount, we kept passing No Vacancy signs at each of the motels. It soon became obvious our only option was to drive straight through to home. I do vaguely remember our two-car caravan stopping

The Musical Messengers — Dad's traveling band. Personnel in this group changed over the period of years. In this photo, left to right, front row: Janet Clemmer, Marlene Styer, Lucy Clemmer, Irma Gahman, Dad. Left to right, second row: Marilyn Halteman, Doris Clemmer, Nancy Heckman, Harold Gahman, Wes Clemmer, Lenny Walter, circa 1960.

at about 2:00 AM and again at 6:00 AM for a bite to eat. Guy and Dad both enjoyed eating, so the excuse of needing food to stay awake served them well.

One other memorable trip to the southland was initiated by Clayton Gotshall. Clayton was from the Souderton area, and had moved to North Carolina for the purpose of planting a mission church. The location he targeted was a rural area not far from Hickory. By the time we made our visit, his church had become a dynamic congregation of about forty or fifty people. This group met for services in a small clapboard building elevated a few feet off the ground by wide brick posts.

Clayton's congregation was a lively Pentecostal church, and our music was effective in igniting their enthusiastic participation. These folks soon had the floor of the building pulsating in rhythmic time with their energetic toe-tapping and hand-clapping. Stirred by their fervor, we began playing and singing with fresh inspiration. It was exhilarating!

The program was scheduled to end at nine o'clock, and our plans were to leave for home immediately afterward. However, as Dad announced the closing song, Clayton insisted that we play just a few more. Those few extra songs stretched into several more. Finally, at ten o'clock, they finally allowed us to end the meeting.

Heading home, we again encountered the No Vacancy dilemma as every motel was filled. Reluctantly, Dad made the decision to do another all-nighter. One consolation that helped make the marathon a bit more tolerable was the clear, beautiful full-moon night. Inspired by the earlier toe-tapping service and strangely wide awake, our ladies' trio, Shirley, Millie, and Wanda sang song after song as we headed north through the night. Their ad-lib concert helped keep Dad awake at the wheel, and also made for a night to remember.

* * *

Though the majority of our Musical Messenger trips took us to southern states, we also had some great experiences in the northlands of Canada.

Irvin Schantz was a Mennonite pioneer who left eastern Pennsylvania to begin a missionary outreach in northern Ontario. Through a series of exploratory initiatives, he eventually targeted a remote wilderness region inhabited by Native Americans of the Ojibway tribe. Steeped in the bondages of godlessness and dysfunctional living, they desperately needed the Gospel. Irvin set up his mission base in Red Lake, a frontier town, literally at the end of the road. His evangelistic efforts began hitting their mark. The Natives responded to Irvin's ministry, and more workers were enlisted to establish multiple outposts throughout those untamed wilds.

Evangelist Harold Fly was a close friend with Irvin. At Irvin's invitation, Harold made periodic trips to Red Lake, conducting evangelistic meetings at the various mission outposts. Harold had a true passion for the work, and actively promoted Irvin's ministry within the Franconia Mennonite Conference. Somewhere along the way, Harold mentioned The Musical Messengers to Irvin.

These Ojibway converts had already been introduced to many of the well-known Christian songs. Harold believed the mission churches would be responsive to Dad's music. As new believers, they had learned the hymns in their own native tongue. Therefore, we would be faced with a communication barrier. But with the universal language of music, these Natives could easily relate to these familiar melodies played instrumentally by our band. Irvin agreed and contacted Dad to make the necessary arrangements.

Our first trip to Red Lake became a reality in the summer of 1958. Preparations for this multi-week tour were a bit more involved than those prior weekend outings. For example, Irvin instructed Dad to have the serial numbers of all our instruments listed on a sheet of paper. This would help eliminate a possible delay when dealing with the Canadian customs officials at the border crossing.

There were no vans in those days. Taking instruments as well as luggage meant Dad had to find a way to fit everything into two sedan cars. He purchased enclosed roof racks for both vehicles. Even with the extra space, every nook and cranny was crammed full with suitcases and instruments. All items had their designated place.

Departure day arrived. Dad had already plotted our travel route, complete with overnight stops along the way. There were some interesting and educational surprises in store for us. At our overnight stop in Windsor, Ontario, a few in our group stayed at a couple's home whose bathroom was an outhouse—a large tree stump. That was definitely a "first" for us.

Continuing on, we arrived in Kitchener, Ontario, at the home of Ed Knechtel. He delighted in showing us through the warehouse of his large wholesale cheese business. Of course, we welcomed the chance to enjoy a good variety of free samples. After leaving Kitchener, we found ourselves driving mile after mile of remote roads bordered by huge expanses of evergreen trees. The scenery was beautiful as we headed north through this wilderness of forests and lakes.

Eventually we came to the Red Lake Road. This route is a well-traveled gravel road that stretches for one hundred miles before ending at the town of Red Lake. Navigating the dusty "endless" highway made us good and ready for the end of our journey. Red Lake was truly a welcome sight. Even today, this mining town is still the end of the road. Cars are unable to travel any further north. The only means of transportation from Red Lake is either dog sled, portaging by boat, or flying by pontoon plane. For us, it felt like we had come to the end of the world.

After settling in at mission headquarters, we began our ministry assignment in this intriguing world. Traveling by float plane and in small boats, we had a new appreciation for what explorers must have experienced navigating these remote areas. We felt privileged to live with the missionaries, interact with the Ojibways, eat moose meat and other unusual foods. This was our first exposure to the foreign mission field. Seeing the needs of these people and realizing the sacrifices missionaries make were enlightening eye-openers. It was an inspiring and life-changing experience.

On the way home, we presented a musical program at a community church in Glendive, Montana. In contrast to the forests and lakes of Ontario, this church was surrounded by vast grain fields and large cattle ranches. Traveling east we made a quick stop at Mt. Rushmore, enjoying the impressive view of this well-known monument of presidents.

The concluding program on our itinerary was a concert at a church in Indiana. By this time, we were happy to think of heading home to good ole' Pennsylvania—travel-weary after 7,000 miles on the road.

Our ministry trips were enriching excursions. Through the years, students who participated would often express how much these encounters were used to shape their lives. The opportunity to interact, travel, and live with Dad and Mom provided a valuable mentoring experience for them. These students became like adopted sons and daughters. Because of the intimate connections forged during our long-distance ministry trips, numerous students enjoyed deep, lasting friendships with Mom and Dad that continued throughout their lives.

24

Evolution of the Clemmer Sound

Even while ministering out of state, Dad's concert focus remained directed to the local annual Souderton event. With a desire to keep enhancing the impact of these larger concerts, Dad began inviting guest musicians to make their contribution as a special feature in the program.

Teaching students outside his Mennonite circle automatically connected Dad with churchgoers from different denominations. Many of these families attended congregations where instrumental music was an accepted expression of corporate worship. Through one of these contacts, Dad found out about accomplished marimba player, Jane Walters. Including a few marimba solos in the program would be a great addition. Dad contacted Jane and she readily agreed to participate. This special feature was an inspiring supplement to the music of Dad's students. People were fascinated with Jane's playing as most had never attended a marimba performance.

Not only were guest musicians added to the program, but another development in Dad's concerts was incorporating new instruments in the band. These additions would contribute significantly to the evolution of "the Clemmer sound."

One day in early January 1953, a new Gibson guitar catalog and price list arrived in the mail. Dad had been fortunate in getting the Gibson franchise, and was doing quite well selling these top-of-the-line guitars. On the back page of this catalog was the picture of a brand new instrument—an electric bass. The body of the EB-Bass Guitar had a violin shape, and the long neck with four strings gave it a distinct look. Immediately Dad was interested, and placed his order for the dark mahogany solid-body guitar.

I [Wes] remember the day it arrived. We eagerly unpacked the long cardboard carton with the familiar Gibson logo. After checking it out visually, we eagerly plugged the bass into the amplifier Dad kept by the sofa in our living room. Wow! What a sound!

Dad had never played a bass, but knew the strings were tuned like the top four strings on a guitar, an octave lower. Being fluent with the bass-chord style of guitar picking with fill-in bass runs, he easily transferred that knowledge and adapted it for bass. Immediately Dad envisioned what a great addition the bass would be to his recital band. He needed to teach someone to play it.

At the time, two Bergey brothers from nearby Lederach were taking lessons. Dad was teaching Dennis on Hawaiian and Paul on Spanish Guitar. At one of Paul's next lessons, Dad let him give the bass a test run. Paul was hooked, becoming the proud owner of that first EB Gibson. With a few pointers from Dad, Paul made the transition to bass and quickly became proficient with this new instrument. That April, our recital band sounded better than ever with the new addition of those low bass notes. Paul became a permanent fixture at his post as "bass man" for several years. He also traveled with us to the Bowery Mission, West Virginia, and all the other places where Dad's Musical Messengers were scheduled to play.

Dennis Goshow was a student of Dad's from Souderton. After developing his abilities on both Spanish and Hawaiian guitar, Denny's interest in bluegrass music set him on a new pickin' pursuit—the five-string banjo. In the late 50s, there was no instruction written for bluegrass banjo. This style of picking had evolved through the creative influences of those gifted to play "by ear."

Denny had an outstanding musical ear, and this ability plus his guitar-pickin experience was all he needed. Denny began teaching himself, sitting in front of the record player. There he learned to copy, note-for-note, the banjo licks on 33 1/3 RPM albums of prominent

The larger concert band at Souderton High School, circa 1954. Marimba player, Jane Walters, is the featured guest artist. Floor microphones between the front stage floodlight panels are connected to tape recorders brought by interested listeners.

pickers like Earl Scruggs, Don Reno and others. To do this, Denny slowed the record down to 16 RPM speed, manually lifting the needle arm and back-tracking to repeat each musical phrase. Though one octave lower in pitch, the slower speed made it easier to hear and repeat the rapid flurry of individual notes. The banjo quickly became Denny's instrumental pursuit.

Though Dad was not teaching Denny at the time, because of the ongoing relationship flowing out of his days as a student, Dad invited Denny to bring his 5-String and participate in the recital band. Without microphone amplification, the acoustic sound of the 5-String was almost lost in the sheer volume of electric guitars and accordions. But the new sound of Denny's banjo was front and center when featured in a vocal bluegrass trio that included me [Wes] on electric bass and Bob Kulp on guitar. Many people liked this bluegrass addition. I was already developing an attraction to banjo music, so playing in the Denny, Wes and Bob trio was key to launching me in my own pursuit of learning bluegrass banjo.

* * *

The instrumental addition that most dramatically transformed our original Clemmer sound was the introduction of brass horns. Prior additions of other string instruments enhanced more than altered it. Trumpets radically changed the familiar sound people had come to identify with Dad and his music. This addition came about in a most interesting way.

As Dad's teaching roster grew, he continued enlisting students from a larger geographical area. Expanding to Spring City, Phoenixville and more distant towns, Dad would devote certain afternoons and evening to those specific areas. As his teaching schedule became maxed out, the only way Dad could foresee making room for more students was to reduce time on the road and begin teaching certain evenings at our house. The Gehman and Shantz families from Bally began coming Mondays after supper. This carload consisted of six or seven pupils, and filled the entire evening for Dad.

A bit later, a carload from the Deep Run and Bedminster area traveled twenty miles to Harleysville for lessons on Thursday evenings.

Harold and Irma Gahman were a brother and sister in that group. Harold wanted to take guitar lessons. He had previously been a trumpet student in the school band, and further developed his playing abilities with private lessons. Harold, better known as Happ, was quite accomplished on trumpet. In the course of weekly lesson-time conversations with Dad, this bit of personal music history came to light.

Adding a trumpet to the guitars and accordions would significantly alter the sound. The idea seemed a bit radical, but certainly worth exploring. Dad really liked Happ, providing additional incentive to make a place for his trumpet. The horn, by its very nature, was loud and able to project well in the midst of the other instruments.

In one sense, it was a bit risky adding the trumpet to our concert band, especially for the conservative Mennonites. Typically, these folks were more accepting of guitar and piano than big band or orchestral instruments. Dad was concerned about the possibility of their reaction, but the strong commitment to follow his heart won out. He was willing to venture the risk.

The creative dimensions of Dad's music-making gift kicked in. He envisioned how a trumpet could uniquely interpret hymns that referenced the scenes of heaven, angelic events and Christ's second coming. He began orchestrating certain songs to feature Happ's horn. Songs like "Onward Christian Soldiers", "At the Battle Front", "When We All Get To Heaven", "Christ Arose" and "Some Bright Morning" became trumpet features. Typically, we would play three stanzas of a song. To highlight the trumpet, Dad arranged one verse for the acoustic string section to provide a rhythm background for the horn solo. Instantly the special arrangements breathed new life into these aged songs.

Harold's trumpet was, in its own way, a pioneering influence. Other band members became interested in horn playing, so Harold began taking on trumpet beginner students. As these developed in their playing ability, more trumpeters were added to the band. The specially arranged hymns featuring trumpets now evolved into multi-part harmonies. People applauded the addition. Their affirmation helped establish horns as a vital part of our Clemmer sound. Something else was permanently established. Harold's special interest in Lucy, my sister, continued blossoming into a serious romance. They eventually married, earning him a permanent place in the band as well as our family circle!

One other feature of those Souderton concerts that became a unique trademark was our theme song. To open the concert, Dad asked one of his Mennonite song-leading peers to lead one or two traditional hymns, sung acappella by the audience. The large stage curtain was closed, with the band waiting anxiously behind it. After the congregational song, Dad would walk out front of the curtain to his Hawaiian guitar mounted on a stand. With his back to the audience, Dad began playing the first notes of "Have Thine Own Way, Lord." The band joined him from the other side of the curtain. At that point, the curtain would begin to slowly open, revealing the large stage filled with musicians. It was quite an impressive experience, helping to set the spiritual tone for the concert that followed.

As time passed, the Clemmer sound continued to evolve. Unique instruments such as the glockenspiel and vibraphone were added. Years later, when grandchildren began emerging on the scene, flute and saxophone brought new sounds to our special arrangements. It was Dad's delight to make room for these additions, fully welcoming that which would improve and creatively enrich what he had birthed.

25

For the Record

The Souderton High concerts were not the only programs Dad presented with the larger band. An unexpected series of events were destined to take these concerts beyond the school auditorium. One new door of opportunity opened through the need for a place to rehearse. As the size of the band continued to grow, we had to find a larger practice facility. Dad shared this need with parents of students, aggressively searching for an open door.

Jack Bechtel's dad, Wesley, was an active member of the Grace EUB church located in Telford. Hearing of Dad's need, he volunteered to check with the board members to see if their fellowship hall would be available. It took a few weeks to process the request, but eventually Wesley was able to report the board's approval. The hall was a good-sized multi-purpose room adjoining the formal sanctuary, and could easily accommodate our large band.

Practices for the spring concert began in February. Every Monday evening, students would arrive and prepare for rehearsal. There was a bee-hive of activity accompanied by a buzz of social interaction. Instruments were removed from cases and the regular task of tuning guitars was begun. In those days we didn't have guitar tuners. Dad would usually tune the first guitar to an accordion, hand the tuned guitar to a "striker" who picked each of the strings, providing the correct pitch as he tuned the next guitar. This went on, instrument after instrument, until all the Hawaiian and Spanish guitars were tuned. Through the years, other experienced guitarists with a developed musical ear replaced Dad in the tuning task.

We were able to rehearse at Telford EUB for many years and maintained a great working relationship with the church. Having the use of this fellowship hall for our practices was a huge blessing. After rehearsing at the EUB facility for a few years, one of the board members contacted Dad with a special request. This representative also served on the board of a Christian campground facility about five miles from Telford along busy Route 309. Highland Park was situated in a large wooded grove with a good number of small summer cottages surrounding a large outdoor pavilion. A main feature of their camp program included sponsoring a variety of inspirational open-air events.

The request presented to Dad was straightforward. Would he consider presenting a program similar to the Souderton concert for one of their summer evening events at Highland Park? Dad was honored by the request, but immediately began considering all the logistics for presenting another large concert. The board didn't mind for the event to be a carbon copy of the April program at Souderton High, which would simplify preparation for Dad. It also eliminated the need to develop an entirely new song list. Though there might be some repeat attenders, the different circle of Highland Park patrons would introduce Dad's music to a group of new listeners. After deliberating and discussing the pros and cons with several others, Dad agreed to go ahead with the plan. He scheduled the first Highland Park recital for a Saturday evening in the middle of June. It turned out to be a beautiful evening. The open-air dynamics added a new dimension to the concert. People driving by could hear the music and come in to enjoy the event.

The stage area of the pavilion was significantly smaller than the school auditorium stage. Fortunately, summer vacation activity prevented a few of the students from participating, so the number of instrumentalists was slightly reduced. Every inch of the platform was jammed with students and their instruments. Music stands were crammed in to every available space. It was almost impossible for musicians to move from their chairs after having taken their places.

The audience seating area held several hundred people. A leafy canopy of woods surrounding the tabernacle provided an overflow listener area for those preferring the comfort of their own lawn chairs. Cottage residents gathered on their porches with a balcony-type vantage point. Others found parking spaces for their cars between the cottages, rolled down their windows and enjoyed the "drive-in" concert. This variety of seating options extended the audience boundaries a good distance beyond the tabernacle. But the immediate under-roof seating brought the primary audience much closer to the band. This provided a brand new dynamic to the concert experience. It afforded a more intimate connection between the performers and listeners than was possible at Souderton High. Several commented to Dad afterward how they preferred the closeness at Highland Park. In future years, they chose to attend that concert rather than the high school event.

At half-time intermission during the first Highland Park concert, a board member came forward to make announcements and receive an offering. After completing these matters of business, he called Dad to the podium to make a presentation. As an expression of appreciation, the board had hired Walter Baghurst, a local sound-recording technician with professional taping equipment, to record the concert. The plan was for Baghurst to produce a 33 1/3 LP record of the concert as a gift for Dad. At that point, the board presented Dad with an empty LP jacket, and announced the finished record would be given to Dad after being produced from the tape recording.

Dad had noticed Walter's taping setup, but thought he was a serious amateur making a personal recording of the evening. In those days, it was not uncommon for persons interested in Christian music or preaching messages to bring reel-to-reel sound recorders and tape those events. This was a normal happening at the Souderton concerts. The band pit in front of the stage was an ideal place for these sound buffs to set up their taping machines and microphones. There could be as many as a dozen recorders lined up for this purpose. Walter's taping gear was somewhat more elaborate than the casual music enthusiast. But Dad's preoccupation with the countless details of pre-concert preparation made him oblivious to Baghurst's assignment.

* * *

This unexpected record presentation from the Highland Park board was a wonderful expression of affirmation for Dad. It also represented the fulfillment of a personal aspiration. As an amateur, Dad had dabbled with cutting the old-style 78 RPM single play vinyl records on a mediocre home machine. He had dreamed of someday being able to record something more professional. Without any further action on his part, God had providentially set the stage and orchestrated the fulfillment of his dream.

Several weeks later, Walter phoned Dad and invited him to stop over to pick up his long-play record. How interesting that Walter's small home studio was located just across the athletic field right next to Souderton High School. Dad enjoyed listening as Walter played a few of the twenty-six "cuts" on his hi-fi studio player.

Of course, the big delight was gathering the family around the walnut cabinet of our living room hi-fi for the first listen. Dad removed the record from the plain red sleeve. There was no photo or liner notes on the jacket describing what the album contained. The round maroon label on the record offered a very sketchy description, imprinted by an ordinary typewriter. The label read: "Annual Sacred Concert—Joseph Clemmer, Director." Each side of the record listed only the first and last song titles with the caption: "Bands arranged in order of program." There were fourteen songs on the first side; twelve on side two. The label also included a few descriptive phrases like "high fidelity" and "uniform frequency response over entire audible spectrum." These claims to sound superiority seem quite amusing when referenced against the fidelity of musical reproduction in our twenty-first century. But in 1954, Dad's first record was a decent quality recording for its time.

* * *

This record added more fuel to Dad's visionary flame. During the months that followed, he continued envisioning the possibility of producing an even better recording of his annual concert. Though Baghurst was hired simply to serve the interests of Highland Park and their desire to bless Dad, the friendship connection birthed through this contact with Walter Baghurst was destined to be the greater gift.

As an audio producer, Baghurst naturally had an eye open for new business opportunities. Dad and his music represented just such a possibility. I would also venture to believe he felt some genuine personal interest in promoting Dad's musical cause. Whatever the motivation for Walter's initiative, in the final analysis, it was providential that he would present Dad with a partnering proposal.

Dad made another trip to Baghurst Audio Productions. There in the midst of reel-to-reel tape recorders, microphones, and the maze of sound cables, they began dialoging about producing albums of future concerts. These records could then be marketed and sold to the growing number of those attracted to the Clemmer sound.

Baghurst seemed enthused about doing a follow-up project. Because the first production was a live recording, it naturally had some inherent limitations. Even in a studio-type recording session, challenges of accurately reproducing the sound of a large variety of instruments needed to be addressed. As Walter and Dad swapped their perspectives from the diverse vantage points of musician and technician, a workable plan began to unfold.

It was decided that one of the Monday evening rehearsals be designated as a recording night. The session would be held in the fellowship hall of the EUB Church. Walter could set up his array of recording equipment and mikes beforehand. Then the band would arrive and perform selected songs in a similar format to the actual concert program. After listening to the master recording, Walter and Dad would make a final selection of the best songs for the actual album.

There was a hubbub of excitement as students began arriving for that first recording session. Some expressed being nervous, hoping they wouldn't make a mistake. Others were a bit unsure, not knowing exactly what to expect. No doubt, Dad was feeling the pressure, hoping to evade unexpected glitches that might mess up the recording. Fortunately for everyone, the initial session went well without any major disruptions.

Afterward, Walter mixed the master recording; then had it pressed and reproduced by one of the commercial record companies he worked with in New York City. He also designed a cover for the jacket, using some creative musical artwork. This was the icing on the cake, giving the finished product a look that equaled albums being marketed by professional musicians of the day.

I can't remember how many records Dad ordered from Baghurst for the 1955 concert. It could have been one hundred or more. Apparently all of them were sold, because we only have one copy of that album. It was a real hit to have records available for sale at the end of the concert. People were able to enjoy this music in their homes and also share it with friends who had not attended the concert. Students delighted in having a copy for themselves, documenting their personal participation in the band. The honor of being "on the record" provided these up-and-coming musicians with a deepened sense of personal accomplishment.

Dad's creative energies would not quit. It wasn't long until he got the idea to have a photo taken of the band and feature it on the front of the album jacket. This picture was a good addition to the yearly record project. The audio sound and a visual picture of adults, teens and younger children with their instruments helped to communicate the uniqueness of our Clemmer Concerts. Band members loved the picture as well, proudly pointing themselves out to their friends. Even today, for recital students, these albums help perpetuate the fond memories associated with this formative experience of music-making.

The annual record project became a major ingredient for the perpetual success of our yearly Souderton High and Highland Park concerts. For fifteen consecutive years, we sold and distributed hundreds of albums. They have been circulated and appreciated from coast to coast in the United States and ended up in foreign countries as well. These albums are a special gift, the sacred sounds of Dad's visionary heart etched in the grooves of vinyl. They provide a tangible legacy to instruct and inspire future generations of young men and women visionaries. God is truly able to accomplish beyond what we can desire or foresee. It is a wonder to watch how He works.

26

Northland Pioneer Adventure

Early morning rays of pink and lavender streamed across the sky as Dad pulled out the lane and headed our Buick down Rt. 113. This was definitely no ordinary excursion as we left town that early August Saturday morning of 1960. Our '59 Electra 225 was probably the largest Buick ever made, but even so it was packed to the hilt. This was the launch of a three-week family vacation and ministry trip—destination Red Lake, Ontario.

Memories of our action-packed trip to Red Lake two years earlier with the Musical Messengers fueled our family's excitement in preparation for this return visit. Anticipation was in the air. The enclosed canvas roof rack was crammed with suitcases and enough clothes for seven. Every inch of the trunk was reserved for instruments—two accordions, an electric bass, a couple of guitars, Dad's Hawaiian guitar, an amplifier, and Wes' trumpet.

Dad was a master packer. It seemed he had a way for creating extra room that didn't exist. Time after time, through the years, it would appear we had too much cargo for the size of our spacious trunk. Inevitably, Dad would eye up the pieces, working with the space until he found the right combination. Sometimes he needed to slam the trunk lid a few times before it finally closed. We would all marvel that every item finally fit.

"I'm aiming to get to Goshen, Indiana, today," Dad remarked as we exited the ticket booth on the Pennsylvania Turnpike and headed west. The day was spent talking, doing crossword puzzles, and checking out the mountains along the turnpike. The seven tunnels in western PA provided a built-in opportunity for us to play our own unique "tunnel game."

I can't remember how this game ever got started. Though it never had a name, a fitting one would have been "keep the beat"—an appropriate game for a musical family. At the very moment our car entered the tunnel, we would begin, in unison, to count aloud, one—two—three—four—five. From that point, we would continue counting quietly, attempting individually to maintain the rhythm established by the group. The instant our car exited the tunnel, we would end our silent count, and each shared their total. It was easy to speed up or slow down, especially in the longer tunnels, counting over the span of a few miles. The aim was all getting the same number, for this is certainly the mark of a good musician—to keep the beat.

That evening after a long, tiring 700 miles of driving, we checked in at a motel with a pool near Goshen College in Elkhart, Indiana. After all those miles on the road, the prospects of an evening swim sounded mighty appealing. "Mother and I will go visit some friends while you children swim," Dad announced. That sounded like a good deal.

The next morning we packed up and headed toward Chicago just as the sun was peeking above the eastern horizon. It seemed a bit odd traveling a long distance on Sunday morning, not participating in a church service. Dad asked Wes to check radio stations and find a program that could serve as our church experience for the day. We did listen to a few broadcasts which helped pass the time.

Shortly after noon, we exited the turnpike, and began heading north. A little while later, Dad broke the silence with a hint of concern in his voice, "I wonder what that bit of swaying is about. I don't think it's roughness in the road." He drove on a bit, locating an appropriate spot to pull off the road bed. Dad and the boys got out to make a quick round-the-car survey. They immediately spotted one of the rear tires about half flat, obviously caused by low air pressure. "It doesn't appear to be a fast leak. I'll see if we can get to a service station," Dad stated, as he got back behind the wheel.

The next few miles we rode in somber silence. There was a mounting level of concern in the air. Here we were, less than two days into our 9,000 mile journey, with the most grueling road conditions yet ahead. What else might we encounter, especially in the last 100-mile stretch of remote dirt road south of Red Lake?

Traveling a few more miles, we silently welcomed the sighting of a service station out ahead. Fortunately, the station had a tire repair shop. It was shut down for the weekend, but our attendant agreed to check the air leak between serving gas customers. After dismounting the wheel and removing the tire, he made a surprise discovery. Calling Dad over, he pointed to the rim. "Your tire's okay. It's your rim—look at this crack!" As Dad inspected the damage, the guy went on. "Man, I've never seen this happen before; maybe it's all that extra weight you're carryin. I don't have a spare rim, and being its Sunday, my supplier is closed." He paused. "It'd be impossible to get one until tomorrow." Dad's idea-wheels were turning. Waiting around till tomorrow was going to be a serious setback. "Could you check with any other stations?" Dad questioned. "Hey, even if I could get a used one, that'd be okay. I really need to get back on the road today if at all possible."

For some reason, the repair guy tuned in to Dad's plea and went the second mile for us. Heading to his desk, he began making some calls. A short while later he was back. "Would you believe, I think we're in luck. A station across town has a used one your size, and he should have it over here within an hour or so." Dad relayed the report to us, and we all celebrated this promising news. A few hours later, the tire and new rim were back in place. Dad paid the bill and we all piled into the car. Heading down the road, it was quite evident we had been unusually blessed. The kindness of the attendant and provision of that used rim seemed beyond mere coincidence. It had to be the favor of the Lord, resourcing us in our time of need.

Though we were deeply grateful, a big question still remained unanswered, especially in Dad's mind. If the wheel problem was caused by our extra heavy cargo, would we have more trouble down the road? It sure didn't make sense to turn around, but was it foolish to keep going? That evening when we stopped at a motel in Wisconsin, Dad remarked, "Even with our setback today, we ate breakfast in Indiana, dinner in Illinois, and supper in Wisconsin. Tomorrow we should make it to a friend in Loman, Minnesota, and then the next day to our destination at Red Lake."

We were on the road again early Monday morning, but lost another couple of hours near Eau Clare, Wisconsin, getting our speedometer repaired. Mom, Lucy, Doris, and I [Jan] went for a long walk. Afterward, we all ate at a McDonalds. This was a novelty for us—hamburgers and thick milkshakes served in just a few minutes for twenty-cents each. Little did we know what a familiar fixture these Golden-Arches would become, circling the globe with their fast-food fare.

Approaching the Canadian border, we were a bit apprehensive about our checkpoint crossing into Ontario. The officer who processed our entry was curt, barking out a bunch of investigative questions. After checking Dad's listing of our musical instruments and asking additional questions about the purpose of our trip, he waved us on. Breathing a sigh of relief, we were thankful that part of our journey was now history. Continuing westward, the landscape began taking on a new look. Large pine forests with lakes of varied sizes became the dominant features. Occasionally, a small cluster of houses or an isolated village dotted the landscape.

Finally, we approached the concluding leg of our journey. Turning off the Trans-Canadian Highway, we headed north on the legendary stretch of dirt road. Though a gravel surface, the roadway was a main thoroughfare, and traffic generally moved at a fair rate of speed. We did encounter a few muddy detours due to road crews repairing rutted stretches of the gravel roadway. The added accumulation of dust and mud on our car now made it difficult to identify the color as green. Here in this wild wilderness of Ontario, we were definitely in the boondocks.

About mid-afternoon, we gladly bid farewell to what felt like an eternal 100 miles. Red Lake was a welcome sight. We relished this reentry into civilization in spite of its crude, mining-town feel. Arriving at the waterfront part of town, it seemed a bit more attractive. Float planes and all manner of fishing boats bobbed up and down, roped to long stretches of bleached wooden docks. This created a picturesque contrast against the sun-sparkling hues of the dark lake waters.

* * *

Upon arrival at the Northern Light Mission headquarters, we were warmly welcomed by a few staff members. Soon, Irvin Schantz came and briefed us on the immediate plans. He and Durrell Hange, another pilot, had the two float planes ready to go. They would be flying our family to the Pecangecumb outpost. After loading our luggage and instruments into the White Cessna and Red Aronka, we found ourselves skimming across Red Lake. Quickly airborne, the pilots had us winging our way over the endless expanse of lakes and forests to our first service.

Pastor Dave and Elva Burkholder were there to greet us as the planes pulled up to their dock. It felt like a touch of home as we sat down to their supper table. Following the meal, we walked along the shore to our first meeting. After our service, Natives came and shook hands with us, showing appreciation for our coming. We realized that a handshake, like a smile, can be understood in any language. A bed at the mission house was a welcome conclusion to the event-filled day.

The next morning, we said good-by to the Burkholders and headed for Poplar Hill, our next destination. With some free time before our evening program, Durrell came up with an attractive proposal. "For those who would like, I'll take you fishing at the rapids. We can also scout out an old graveyard on the way to the river." That sounded like a great plan. In no time we had changed our clothes and were following Durrell along the narrow well-worn path carved upon the dense forest floor.

After several minutes he turned aside, pointing to a small clearing containing a number of the Native graves. As we gazed at the strange box-like structures, Durrell explained, "Notice the top of the grave looks like a small doghouse, and look at the charms and beadwork at the door. They provide these trinkets to chase evil spirits away from the graves of their loved ones." As we stood gazing at this strange burial site, it all felt rather creepy.

Continuing on our way, Durrell pointed out the large garden of beans, carrots, and other vegetables planted by the missionaries. "Even

One of our musical programs among the Indians of the Canadian northlands. Irvin Schantz, founder of Northern Lights Gospel Missions, and our pilot, is in the foreground.

though the growing season is short they work hard to raise sizable quantities of their own food," he informed us. "This helps reduce the amount of food needing to be flown in from the outside."

Fishing at the rapids was definitely a highlight, especially for Wes and Dean. In no time we had an impressive string of Pike and Walleye, a fitting climax to this entertaining outing. Too soon, it was time to return for our service at Poplar Hill. By the time we finished our concert and were again airborne, it was beginning to feel like a music-making marathon.

Deer Lake turned out to be one of our favorite stops. Director Alvin and Lydia Fry were engaging hosts, and our ministry with their growing congregation seemed extra special. We began our meeting in the log chapel, but when it grew dark inside, we moved outside with our instruments. That far north, summer sunsets take place between ten and eleven o'clock. These Natives kept asking for more music and were in no hurry to leave. Unable to speak in a common tongue, our communication through the universal language of music felt unusually intimate. What an intriguing picture—pale-faced Pennsylvanians and copper-toned Canadian Ojibways joined together in spirit by the old-time hymns of the traditional Christian church. Finally the Native crowd dispersed, just as a vigorous summer shower arrived. That night, we fell asleep to the sound of steady rain dancing on the roof of the rugged mission outpost. This was truly another world.

The next morning we didn't fly to MacDowell because of the threatening weather. Instead, we put our time to good use joining Alvin on a foot trip to a real-life Ojibway trading post. This place was a beehive of activity as tribal people converged to do their "in-town" business. Finally the weather improved and we were cleared for takeoff. After a bunch of warmhearted good-bys, we headed for Sandy Lake, our next stop. The Sandy Lake experience was destined to be our most dramatic.

* * *

After supper with Henry Hostetter and his wife, we headed for our next service. It was to be held in a small Ojibway settlement several miles from the mission outpost. Durrell took Mom and our instruments in the airplane. The rest of us went by boat and then walked single-file on a narrow path. It led through a dense stretch of damp, insect-infested forest. The mosquitoes were terrible! We could actually see them swarming around the head of the person in front of us. Doris, Lucy, and I put bandannas on to protect us, and Dad put a hankie over his head. In addition to the mosquito problem, we realized our guide, Mrs. Hostettler, was not sure of her directions. My nineteen-year-old mind mused, "Here we are way back in the middle of nowhere, and now we're uncertain which way to go. What a risky adventure!" Little did I know how adventurous this outing was about to become.

Fortunately, we did choose the right path and soon came to a familiar landmark for our guide—the home of the local Catholic priest. "I'm glad you're with me," Mrs. Hostetter remarked, "because the priest has been giving us trouble. Some months ago the boys' quartet from Christopher Dock School was here to sing, and he stopped them from having their meeting. Several days ago the priest also stole our boat. Fortunately, the Natives got it back for us. Since then, they've not been on good terms with him."

As we digested her report along with the hostile implications, it was obvious we needed God's divine intervention for that evening. Dad agreed to go ahead with the meeting as planned. He had faith God would make a way for us. We set up outside one of the local huts some distance from the priest's house, and were ready to begin.

Durrell opened the service with Bible reading and prayer. About the time his prayer ended, the priest stormed into our circle and began angrily ranting and raving. He gave no hint of heeding Durrell's appeals, insisting we cease the meeting immediately. This was Catholic territory, and we were trespassing on his staked-out claim of holy ground. Suddenly a Native strode up front, shaking his fist in the priest's face. Meanwhile, we sat there wide-eyed, not sure what to make of this impromptu fight. Durrell calmly told the priest that the Natives requested the meeting, and we needed to proceed or it would soon be dark.

At this point, Dad was tempted to just begin playing our first song. But immediately a follow-up impression came—to use another approach. Instead, Dad asked the priest if he would listen to just one song. The priest paused momentarily, and then mumbled gruffly, "Okay!" Immediately, we launched into our theme song, "Have Thine Own Way, Lord." Let me tell you, we never sang that prayer with any more fervency. Suddenly and without warning, we had been thrust into the middle of a spiritual battle, and were counting on the intervening power of God to have His way—to save the day.

We always played the song instrumentally and sang two verses. On this occasion, we took the liberty to sing all four verses, extending the song to its ultimate length. With every verse, Dad's faith increased. At the song's conclusion, without hesitation, he boldly led us into song number two. Surprisingly, we were permitted to continue, with one song following the next. Our hearts were greatly stirred as we sensed the spirit of God orchestrating the service and working in the hearts of those around us.

At one point the priest took off his hat and actually began singing with us. After the meeting he came forward and shook hands, expressing his affirmation of our ministry. Never before had we witnessed such visible evidence regarding the power of musical worship in confronting and overcoming the powers of spiritual opposition. We were reminded of the biblical account when David's harp became an instrument of spiritual breakthrough in confronting the evil spirits tormenting King Saul. It was an incredible experience.

As we prepared to leave, the winds began to pick up. Glancing upward, we scanned the bank of storm clouds racing across the sky. "Since the water is so choppy right now, I can only take a few of you at a time," Durrell informed us. I'll need to make a couple trips. The priest stood nearby, overhearing our dilemma. He stepped forward, directing his proposal to Durrell. "Why don't you bring the boat over to my dock and launch from where the water is likely not as rough," he offered. We immediately accepted his proposition.

Having won the favor and respect of the priest, Dad was inspired to join him. Together they traipsed through the woods toward his dock. Side by side these two men walked, greatly discordant in so many ways, and yet strangely harmonized through the reconciling power of the Gospel. The Word in song had won the day. It transformed that plot of wilderness soil into holy ground. What long-term effect might our encounter have on this dear man's life? Only God could answer that question in His time and His way.

While we were waiting at the dock, the priest offered to take us back home with his boat. However, just as he was suggesting this, the missionary boat arrived to ferry us across the waters. Our hearts welled up in praise to God for changing the heart of the priest. He had directed and protected us in the spiritual challenges of the evening. It was a profound faith lesson for us all—one we would rehearse over and over again.

27

Celt Lake Crisis

Airplanes and Northern Light Gospel Mission represent an inseparable partnership. The only practical way to traverse the woods-and-water wilderness between mission headquarters and the various outposts is by planes equipped with float devices. In the summertime, pontoon floats allow these planes to take off and land on the vast network of lakes. In the winter, pontoons are replaced with skis, enabling aircraft to navigate from land to air from the frozen bodies of water.

As our family traveled from outpost to outpost giving programs, we gained a first-hand appreciation for just how important these small planes are to the missionaries. Transporting large quantities of supplies by air is a normal, every-day part of the work. Weight limits for these small aircraft are crucial, since take-offs from the water offer greater resistance than from land. The mission pilots conscientiously abided by these weight guidelines, but the two planes transporting our family, luggage, and instruments were pretty well loaded to the max.

Sunday morning we finished our service at Bemudji. Grabbing a quick lunch, we headed for the lakeside dock in preparation for our one-hour flight to Grassy Narrows. It was a glorious sunny afternoon. Billowy white clouds dotted the stunning blue sky. With barely a breath of breeze, the lake was practically motionless.

As Durrell was fueling the smaller plane and performing his routine preflight checks, Irvin cranked up the larger Cessna. In no time he had

Dad and Mom along with Doris and Lucy airborne. They soon disappeared out of sight. By this time Durrell had the red Aeronca about ready for take-off. Wes helped him load the accordion and two guitars in the plane. I [Jan] crawled in the back with Dean. Wes strapped himself in the front passenger seat alongside Durrell.

With a turn of the switch, the engine roared to life. We slowly taxied out from the dock to position ourselves for departure. After a gradual turn, Durrell gunned the engine and we skimmed across the lake, accelerating for lift-off. We could not get airborne. The combination of our maxed-out load and the absence of a headwind was restricting our take-off. Durrell circled back, making a second attempt from a slightly different angle, but with no success. If only the other plane was still present, we could possibly reapportion the load.

Circling back for our third attempt, all of us prayed under our breath, asking the Lord for some extra lift assistance from a few angels. Again, Durrell gunned the engine as pontoons whizzed across the placid lake. Finally, we felt the plane break free from the surface of the water and begin to climb. The altimeter registered our gradual ascent to 500 feet, then 800 feet and beyond. Gazing out the window at the receding trees now dwarfed below, I breathed a silent sigh of relief and thanksgiving.

In the co-pilot seat, Wes was being entertained by the flight talk transmitted through the extra pair of headphones Durrell had allowed him to use. He was also absorbed in the flight map. It provided comprehensive topographical information about the entire region. Meanwhile, the drone of the whirling propeller was acting as a lullaby for Dean. With his head on my lap, he was soon fast asleep.

We settled in at our cruising speed and altitude. I occupied myself with soaking in the intriguing panorama of woods, water, and endless sky. It stretched in all directions, as far as the eye could see. What awesome magnificence!

At about that time, the monotonous drone of the engine was suddenly interrupted with a very slight stutter. Instantly it again returned to the original monotone sound. A few minutes later, it happened again. This "stutter" repeated another time or two, but with less space between the interruptions. Durrell maneuvered the fuel mixture knob,

Flight checks and fueling of airplanes in preparation for our trip to the Pecangecumb outpost. Location is the headquarters of Northern Lights Gospel Missions.

and that adjustment seemed to momentarily improve the aircraft's performance. But in a short time, the stutter would be repeated. It was evident the knob adjustment would not be a lasting fix.

I was not in a position to observe Durrell's facial expression. Even so, I surmised by his posture in the cockpit that concern about this malfunction was mounting. He turned his head toward Wes, who was looking his direction, searching for some reassurance that all was okay. Above the roar of the engine, Durrell finally transmitted his verdict into words. "I think I know what the problem is," he acknowledged. "A few months ago, one of the other pilots had a similar problem with this plane. In that case, the fuel filter screen had gotten dirty, restricting the flow of gasoline to the engine." Durrell paused for a moment and then continued his assessment. "I've not worked on this engine before, but if I can keep it running well enough to land the plane, I should be able to clean the filter. Hopefully that will fix our problem."

Glancing over to his side window, Durrell searched the landscape below. Then he turned to Wes and said, "We could go back to Ear Falls, but I don't know if we can make it that far. Wes, you've been following our progress on the air map. Check to the left of our present location. You should see a smaller-sized body of water—a lake. Does it have a name?" Wes took several moments to orient himself, and while pointing his finger to reference the landmark exclaimed, "Yea, that must be Celt Lake."

Immediately, Durrell began a gradual circling descent, his eyes fixed on our proposed landing sight. "Because of the lower water levels due to our dry summer, I'm really concerned about landing in an unfamiliar area," he said, a touch of sober misgiving in his voice. "There is always the threat of an unseen rock or debris just below the surface of the water. If so, it could rip the pontoon during our landing. That's why we do our best to avoid landing in uncharted waters," he informed us. "But this is an emergency, and we have no other choice. I'm gonna try it."

Durrell grabbed his radio mike and began broadcasting his identification number and location. We listened intently as he informed any other pilots within range that we were preparing for an emergency landing. Durrell also requested anyone hearing this message to notify mission headquarters at Red Lake about our urgent situation.

Now, down within a few hundred feet of the lake, Durrell banked the plane as he circled one more time. He did his best to scan the lake surface, intent on making our forced landing a safe one. By this time, Dean was wide awake. "Are we there now?" he questioned. Putting on the best motherly voice possible, I explained what had happened, assuring him everything would be okay.

My earlier feelings of excitement about this adventure were now being overrun by an increased array of anxieties. "I'm the only girl! Will we have to stay overnight? What if Durrell's diagnosis is wrong? Are there savage Natives around?" An acute sense of apprehension filled the aircraft as Durrell cautiously guided the plane into our final descent. It seemed like an eternity until the slight thud of pontoons touching water triggered a brief tremor throughout the cabin. Yea! We were down safe and sound.

Durrell had spied a small beach over on the east side of the lake. We taxied to that sandy strip and pulled up the Aeronca close to shore. Shutting off the plane, Durrell flipped open the door and crawled out onto the pontoon. Jumping into the shallow waters, he and Wes pulled the aircraft onto the beach.

With a small ax from the cockpit, they chopped some smaller limbs from trees to lay across the pontoons. This provided a platform to stand on while exploring the engine problem. With the anxieties of our forced landing now behind us, the sense of adventure quickly returned. Wes exclaimed, "Just think, we may be the first white men that ever set foot in these parts!" Dean and I walked further up the beach to do a bit of exploring.

Durrell soon had the red engine cover removed and handed it to Wes. "If you hear a plane, Wes," he instructed, "wave the cover so they can see it. The army may have picked up my emergency call and come looking for us."

* * *

Meanwhile there was grave concern at Grassy Narrows. Our plane was long overdue, and the prospects didn't look good. Knowing that Durrell was a relatively new pilot, it stood to reason he may have drifted off course and gotten lost. Running out of fuel was another risk. No one wanted to entertain the thought of the worst possible scenario. A crash due to an aircraft malfunction was a daily threat. If this was our fate, the search in the wilds of this untamed wilderness would literally be of the needle-in-the-haystack variety.

Norman Schantz, brother to Irvin, was the lead missionary at Grassy Narrows. He and Dad discussed the likelihood of various possibilities. Irvin busied himself preparing the white Cessna for an emergency search-and-rescue mission. It was time for the afternoon service to begin. A cluster of Natives had already gathered for the special event. How could the Clemmer family minister with half its members missing?

The ignition of Irvin's Cessna abruptly broke in, momentarily interrupting Dad and Norman's dialog. The roar afforded Dad an opportunity to ponder the severity of this crisis with some soul-searching self-talk. There's no telling what all he processed with conscious thought, but a deep-crying unto-deep dialog was definitely at work within him.

Scrambling in a frantic attempt to find a foothold for his faith, Dad's mind must have rambled back over the years. He likely recalled past adversities and daunting adversaries that posed varied threats to his life, his work, and his ministry. But all former crisis experiences paled in comparison to this one. Though many of those obstacles had seemed impossible at the time, none had threatened to destroy multiple members of his precious family. How ironic this threat should occur right in the midst of such glorious fulfillment of his ultimate life dream—to be on the front lines of pioneering ministry, utilizing his God-given gift of musical praise, surrounded by his family partnering with him. Why would God allow this menacing intrusion? Would the circle be unbroken?

The noise of the departing plane became a distant drone as Norman's question terminated Dad's internal musings. "Shall we go ahead and start the meeting? My son, Roy has a guitar you can use." Dad agreed, all the while feeling incapable of pushing aside a hoard of anxious thoughts about the missing children. After some introductory remarks and the opening prayer, Norman turned the service over to Dad. With heavy hearts, Doris and Lucy joined him with our "well-worn" theme song, "Have Thine Own Way, Lord." This favorite had never been more difficult to sing. However, as they moved through the verses, the words seemed to ignite a spark of fresh faith in the sovereign God—the One who orchestrates His plans of welfare and not calamity, to give His children a future and a hope.

* * *

Back at Celt Lake, the troubleshooting task was fully under way. Durrell was accessing the fuel line assembly, and with some clean gas, had carefully washed the filter. As he reassembled the line, Durrell hopefully exclaimed, "I pray that does it!"

Wes, returning from his own treasure-hunting adventure, was carrying a weathered two-foot piece of driftwood. "Isn't this neat!" he exclaimed. "I'm gonna take it along for a remembrance of our forced landing at Celt Lake." Hopefully, Dad would consent.

With the engine cover again in place, Durrell and Wes removed the make-shift work platform. We reboarded the Aeronca and fastened our seatbelts. Durrell started the engine, pulled out of the cove and into open waters, preparing for take-off. Glancing over at Durrell, Wes noticed beads of perspiration glistening on his forehead. The ultimate test was yet ahead. Was the filter fix the ultimate fix needed to take us safely to our destination?

Thanks to some headwind, we were quickly airborne and on our way. Because of the extended delay, Durrell made the decision to fly directly back to Red Lake headquarters. He knew Irvin was likely in the air initiating his own search effort. Durrell was on his radio, persistently attempting to make contact. Again and again he called, wanting to assure Irvin of our safety. Finally he heard what sounded like a barely audible response from Irvin's radio. He was likely on the very fringes of our broadcasting range. Without giving any details, Durrell announced we were safe and headed back to Red Lake. Through the static, there seemed to be a faint acknowledgment from Irvin that the message was received. At that point, we lost contact.

Our plane buzzed along without any problem. Thank God! I felt a renewed sense of joy at the first sight of Red Lake in the distance. As our aircraft circled and started descending, we could see a group of people gathered at the dock, anxiously awaiting our touch-down. We found out later that Irvin had sent an SOS call to Kenora requesting they notify mission headquarters in Red Lake about the missing plane. The staff had been called together for an impromptu prayer vigil, interceding fervently for our safe return. Needless to say, they were overjoyed to see us—the living proof of God's glorious answer to their fervent prayers.

* * *

Fortunately, Irvin's radio did pick up our transmission that we were okay and headed back to Red Lake. When he returned to Grassy Narrows with the good news, the rest of the family had just completed their musical program. You can imagine the outburst of joy that erupted from deep within their hearts.

After a brief meal and warm good-bys, the Cessna was winging its way back to Red Lake. All passengers were fully occupied with the glorious prospects of a memorable family reunion. What a memorable reunion it was—a wonderful blend of warm hugs mingled with free-flowing tears. As we recounted the amazing events of the day, we praised God for bringing us back safely together as a complete family.

It was a day for our family to remember and relive many times in the years to come. Though there's no way of knowing for sure, it seems this experience was likely ordained by God to help deepen "the tie that binds" in our family. Going through a crisis together does tend to have a forging effect in relationships.

Time has a way of dimming the drama of that memorable day. However, a mere mention of the Celt Lake experience still triggers a vivid sense of gratitude for this special faith lesson God taught the Clemmer family in the midst of our action-filled northland adventure.

28

The Business Boom

Living along Harleysville Pike, we must have passed by Stan Hackman's electrical appliance store thousands of times. Only a mile up the road on our way to Souderton, it looked like a rather impressive establishment through the eyes of a boy. Stan's spread included living quarters, store showroom, repair shop, and parking lot.

As a progressive businessman with a double dose of personal charisma, Stan's business mushroomed. Growth in sales positioned him to begin purchasing appliances from wholesalers in larger quantities. A sizeable warehouse was needed to house the increase of on-hand inventory, so Stan had one built behind the store. This large brick-front structure designed with a loading dock to accommodate tractor trailer shipments added significantly to the visible size of the place.

Dad would occasionally stop in at Hackman's Electric. Usually it was to purchase light bulbs, home appliances or related electrical items. He and Stan were old school buddies, and their talk would always include a healthy round of socializing. Like Dad, Stan had a great sense of humor. I [Wes] often tagged along with Dad and got to eavesdrop on their chats. Their witty and light-hearted kidding was great entertainment.

It was in the midst of these spontaneous conversations that Stan occasionally gave voice to his future game plan. With two daughters involved in other pursuits and no sons, the chance of passing on the business to a family successor did not exist. So, Stan dreamed of eventually selling Hackman's Electric, moving to Florida, and retiring there. Hearing Stan's plan got Dad's visionary mind rolling. Boldly, he would formulate his dream into words. "Stan, when you get ready to sell this place, don't forget, I want first chance to buy it."

Over the years, Dad continually added fuel to the fire of his dream to own that property. Over and over again he would rehearse that dream while passing Hackman's store on our frequent trips to Souderton. "That sure would make a great music store!" Though it was somewhat larger than what he needed at the time, Dad's pioneering mind was looking into the future. This prime location with great visibility could help provide the base for expanding his own business pursuits. Though Stan's dream of selling and Dad's dream of buying were frequently expressed, time passed without a clear sense of when this transaction would ever become reality.

With my first-hand exposure to the dream phase of this potential deal, I missed out on the actual closing of the transaction. At the time, I was newly married and completing a two year term of alternate military service in New Hampshire. With a desire to return home after completing my assignment, I was elated when the news came. Dad was radiant as he shared the news with me. "Stan is selling the store, and we have come up with an agreement to buy it!"

After completing the deal, Dad wasted no time in contacting architect, Ves Tyson. The front store portion required little alteration. However, a new floor plan for the large repair department was needed to serve the unique needs of a music store. When Mr. Tyson came back with the preliminary sketch, Dad was shocked to see five studio teaching rooms included in the layout. "I don't need five!" Dad exclaimed. "Two or three will be enough; one for me, one for Wes, and maybe another for a piano teacher." Ves smiled. "In six months, you will be making good use of all five." Years later, Dad would make occasional reference to that discussion. How grateful he was for listening to the word wisely spoken through his friend, Ves. What a gift to have someone with a prophetic sense, able to envision that which went beyond what he himself was then able to dream.

Dad had enlisted a deer hunting buddy, Harold Mininger, to do the store renovations. Grand opening week was quite a marathon.

Mininger and his crew were busy putting the finishing touches on their remodeling work. Mom and others who served as the cleaning crew followed close behind. At the same time, we were fully engaged in transporting guitars, organs and all the other instruments from Dad's house to the store. The new shipment of pianos needed to be tuned. It was a monumental job, and the Friday deadline was fast approaching. Could we be ready in time?

What a surprise and delight to have Harold and Lucy show up. They had secretly planned to surprise us by traveling all the way from Pueblo, Colorado, arriving just in time to be on hand for the big event. We were overjoyed! They immediately jumped in to the action and helped us tackle all the last minute tasks needing to be completed.

Celebration Friday was quite a memorable day. Radio Station WBYO was on hand with a mobile studio, broadcasting live on the parking lot right by the store. Guest professional musicians provided instrumental entertainment to help enhance the festive atmosphere. The community showed up in mass to check it all out. People affirmed what they saw, delighted to have a sizable full-line music store close by. New inquiries for music instruction began to immediately pour in. Quickly we transitioned from a simple in-house operation to a bustling full-line music store business. Harold and Lucy moved home from Colorado several months later. Beginning as a part-time teacher, Harold gradually transitioned into a full-time partner with Dad and me.

Dad's German work ethic was instrumental in structuring those early days at the store. We opened the doors bright and early at eight o'clock each morning of our six-day week. Wednesdays and Fridays were thirteen-hour marathons. By the time six o'clock on Saturday evening rolled around, we were good and ready to close shop. Sunday was a welcome break.

The season from Thanksgiving to Christmas was especially grueling. As with many other retail businesses, a large percentage of yearly sales are made during those four weeks, driven by Christmas gift buying. Dad wanted to make sure we were taking full advantage of this opportunity to make extra sales. Our evening hours extended to nine o'clock all six days of the week.

The front showroom of our store facility located on Rt. 113 between Harleysville and Souderton, PA. As a full-line music store, anything musical is for sale. In the early to mid-1970s (the era of these photos), pianos, organs, guitars, drums and sound reinforcement equipment represented the largest portion of our sales.

I shared Dad's desire to see the business succeed, but became increasingly concerned about not having time for my family and other recreational interests. Customers rarely showed up at the early morning hour of eight o'clock. Why not open the store at a later time? Also, what about a day off for each of us? With three to share the load, we should easily be able to cover for one another. Harold stood with me in making our appeal.

The idea of taking a day off other than Sunday was quite challenging to Dad's farm-work orientation. While initially resisting our proposal, he finally agreed. Although not embracing the day-off concept with our level of conviction, he gradually came to better understand how it helped Harold and me fulfill our fathering responsibilities. Working through this difference was one of the early tests that helped shape our capacity to work together as a team. It was a valuable lesson, learning to exercise the healthy discipline of give and take.

* * *

The late 1960s and early 1970s were a real hay-day for Clemmer Music. With the ongoing flow of students enrolling for lessons, we were continually on the lookout for qualified teachers who could help provide instruction. After school hours were especially busy. At times, we needed to utilize the repair shop for a teaching studio because all five rooms were filled.

The great location along busy Route 113 provided the store with high visibility. With the community's steady growth and the constant influx of new people moving in, people inevitably came to know about Clemmer Music. A strong retail business fed by both walk-in customers and students needing instruments enabled us to acquire a number of name-brand franchises and offer high quality instruments at competitive prices.

During the early 1970s, the interest in electronic home organs was at its peak. We were fortunate to secure two of the top organ franchises, and this part of our business grew rapidly in just a few years. Because of having a sizable warehouse, we were able to do strategic buying and stock a good variety of instruments to offer customers. On one particular occasion we purchased an entire tractor-trailer load of fifty-two Conn organs in one shipment, direct from the factory.

This organ company also offered incentive reward travel for dealers that purchased a certain annual dollar volume. We were fortunate in being able to win those free vacations for several consecutive years, and took turns traveling to places like Hawaii, Rome, Paris, and Acapulco. This was a welcome bonus, helping to compensate for the sacrificial investments required when owning and operating a flourishing family corporation.

Another fulfilling aspect of the business was helping to provide quality musical instruments for missionaries. We were able to befriend and help church planters and evangelists who literally took our instruments around the world. Some of the larger ones were crated and shipped to foreign countries. In many ways, the business had become a ministry.

In 1977 I felt impressed to terminate my involvement as a partner in the business with a desire to transition into pastoral ministry. This was difficult for Dad to accept, though he and Mom were gracious and supported us in our move. I know his dream would have been for me to continue partnering with Harold to manage the business after he retired. As Dad was processing my decision to leave, I wonder if he thought back to his own career choice years earlier. The dynamics would have been similar to when he stepped away from the family farm to follow his sense of call in music. Over time, Dad was able to make the adjustment, actually affirming that I had done the right thing. Eventually Dad officially retired, but continued helping at the store as long as he was able. Since that time, Harold has carried on the business and done a wonderful job of serving the musical interests of the region.

29

Extending and Ending

The ripple effect and expanding impact of Dad's concerts did not end with Highland Park. Visionaries stimulate vision in other visionaries. A vision birthed in the heart of a plain Mennonite girl was destined to export our larger concerts to a neighboring county.

It happened at the close of our 1962 Highland Park concert. As the crowd was beginning to exit the pavilion, a group of four young ladies from Lancaster were also preparing to leave. Irene Deiter, one of the girls, suddenly spoke up, "I'm going up there to meet Mr. Clemmer!" The other three told Irene they were not particularly interested, and would wait for her at the back of the pavilion. Irene made her way up the center aisle and eventually caught Dad's eye. He came over to the railing at the edge of the platform. After introducing herself and expressing appreciation for the concert, Irene launched into her brainstorm proposal. Would Dad consider bringing the concert to Lancaster County?

Irene had more than a casual interest in Dad's music. Though having grown up in the Mennonite church with a heritage of non-instrumental worship, like Dad, she was infatuated with a love for guitar music. At the time, she was taking Hawaiian guitar lessons from Robert Mooney, a teacher in the Lancaster area.

The concert experience had been an inspirational encounter for Irene. She needed to make a way for others in her region to share the blessing as well. Dad listened intently as Irene presented her proposal. It included the novel idea of hosting Dad's concert outdoors on the lawn beside her home. Irene lived with her widowed mother along the main street of Strasburg, a quaint town near the heart of Amish country. Irene continued on with her enthusiastic pitch. "Maybe you could bring a smaller group of your best players. And I'm sure Mother would agree to help me prepare a meal for your band prior to the concert."

Knowing there was already a significant following from that area, it seemed reasonable for Dad to consider the possibility. On the other hand, a home setting naturally had some limitations, and the logistics of setting up for even twenty to twenty-five players on an open lot would be quite a task. "We'll pray about it," was Dad's immediate reply.

Through a series of phone calls and planning discussions, the Strasburg concert was birthed into being. The band was trimmed down in number to approximately sixteen musicians. Irene contacted John Eby from Christian radio station WDAC. His assistance in helping with promotional and advertising detail was representative of others who partnered with Irene to fulfill her vision.

That early September evening of 1963 was ideal for the concert. After a cafeteria-style meal for the band followed by our typical set-up and tuning rituals, people began to arrive. An audience of 300-400 occupied lawn chairs, blankets and folding chairs provided by the local fire hall. Some listened from their cars parked along both sides of the street. It was a great evening.

Afterward, a few of Irene's girlfriends took her aside and asked, "Are we going to do it again?" Irene had already been pondering that question. Their coaxing provided all the more reason to explore the possibility. It would be worth pursuing, especially if a school facility could be secured. The uncertainty of weather along with all the extra administrative detail needed to pull off an outdoor event could be eliminated. A sizable auditorium would provide room for larger crowds and offer adequate parking. Irene decided that if the facility was available, she would pursue, with Dad, the idea of an annual Lancaster concert.

The logical place to begin her exploration was the local Lampeter-Strasburg High School. Fortunately, Irene had a good friend who worked in the office. Through this contact, Irene set up an appointment to present her request to the school business manager. On the day of her scheduled meeting, she headed for the high school. With a prayer on her lips and hope in her heart, Irene entered Mr. Campbell's office toting the latest Clemmer Concert album from her collection.

After a few introductory remarks, Irene launched into her presentation. Mr. Campbell was intrigued. She handed him the record album. After scanning the jacket cover photo and briefly reading the written copy, he looked up again. With a twinkle in his eye, Campbell gestured toward Irene and exclaimed with a touch of humor, "The powers that be are working to remove the Bible out of the school, and here you are proposing to bring it back in."

Mr. Campbell's favor was a great asset. It wasn't long before Irene received word that approval was granted for hosting the concert at the school facility. Beginning in 1964, this became our yearly fall Lancaster County concert. It grew significantly in numbers. From the beginning, Dad decided to make it a benefit concert. At the time, he and a few other mission-minded businessmen were helping to resource Irwin Schantz and the missions work of Northern Lights Gospel Mission. Each year, they made contacts to raise funds and secure food to fill a tractor trailer and transport the goods to Red Lake. Funds from offerings received at the fall concert were a great asset to the Red Lake mission project. The benefit element added a meaningful dynamic to our yearly Lampeter-Strasburg event.

*　*　*

For a number of years after 1964, we presented three annual concerts—the spring concert at Souderton High School, the summer concert at Highland Park, and the fall concert at Strasburg. These musical events were a wonderful incentive for the growing number of students, and a great promotion for our music store. But the concerts also required a considerable amount of time investment and additional work. The practices, the yearly album production and the actual con-

In latter years, back home again for a family jam session, complete with in-laws. Clockwise, from far left: Dad (lap steel), Wes (banjo), Dean (pedal steel), Doris (accordion), Leonard, her husband (accordion), Harold, husband of Lucy (acoustic guitar), Verna, wife of Wes (acoustic guitar), Janet's (accordion), Lucy, just beyond the photo, but a very vital part (electric bass). A very precious memory!

certs themselves became increasingly challenging for us to schedule between the ever-increasing demands of the business and our growing families.

Upon entering the early 1970s, Harold and I began to discuss with Dad the possibility of discontinuing the Souderton High and Highland Park concerts. It was certainly understandable that Dad would wrestle with this prospect. The recitals had become such a fulfilling part of his life. They had also been used in a profound way to motivate and advance hundreds of students in their personal musical development. In addition to these benefits, thousands of people who attended the recitals had been blessed and enriched in countless ways.

Against the backdrop of these blessings was the deepening realization of another life reality—seasons change. Down deep, Dad understood this law. Throughout his life, he had again and again operated in the changing season principle. As a pioneer, Dad was graced to embrace the maxim: "We cannot reach for the future if our hand is chained to the past." But in letting go, there was no clear sense of what he was reaching for. What could match the level of joy and fulfillment connected to those concert experiences?

On the surface, Dad appeared to make the shift rather well. Increasing demands of the business provided the practical reality that enabled him to let go. Also, continuing the Strasburg concert for a few more years helped ease the sense of loss. Even with these compensations, closing this chapter had to be among the most traumatic events Dad ever encountered. At the time, I doubt he was in touch with the heart-grief it caused. But today, as I step back in time to reflect upon this era of Dad's life, I truly believe when the Souderton and Highland Park concerts were put to rest, a part of Dad died with them—as a grain of wheat falls into the earth.

30

Sunset Years

Sunsets are spectacular to behold. The stunning pinks and purples or glowing oranges are artistically blended. Each creation displays its own unique beauty. While providing a dramatic climax to daylight, sunsets gradually fade. The measured transition from light to darkness marks the passing of another day. Work is concluded. The day is complete.

Those sunset years of Dad and Mom's life were a mixed bag. The pleasure of keeping up with ten grandchildren was certainly a crowning glory during their latter days. They continued enjoying the countless opportunities to love and be loved within their large circle of close friends. Vacations to faraway places like South America, Japan, and China helped satisfy Dad's perpetual itch to travel. Mom kept busy with her ministry of encouragement through her numerous cards and letters, her shoo-fly cupcakes in recycled shredded-wheat boxes, and her faithfulness in prayer. She would often give a magnet, a mug, or other small gifts, bringing cheer to needy individuals. These and many other enjoyments for Mom and Dad made up the colorful palette of their sunset years.

Against this radiant backdrop, some disquieting shades of darkness began to appear. These adversities presented themselves in the form of health challenges. Mom developed a heart condition requiring the implantation of a pacemaker. At the time, these heart-assisting devices were an emerging technology. Mom encountered her

Dad and Mom in the prime of their golden years. What a treasure to remember them this way—in love with life and one another!

fair share of complications as malfunctioning implants were replaced with upgraded versions. Fortunately, this physical limitation did not seriously restrict her activity. Mom was able to continue her loving acts of service. She remained relatively productive until the last days of her life.

For Dad, it was a different story. During his early seventies, it gradually became apparent something peculiar was at work in his body. Dad's voice, normally strong and resonant, began to weaken. His stride, typically aggressive, was marked by the slightest bit of a shuffle. These symptoms can sometimes be the consequence of normal aging. In Dad's case, an extensive examination pointed to a disappointing medical diagnosis—Parkinson's Disease.

This was sobering news to us all. Dad had always been the tower of strength. Through the years, he had a proven track record of successfully overcoming insurmountable obstacles that crossed his path. But, barring a miracle, this physical invader represented an opponent he would not have the ability to conquer.

Fortunately for Dad and us, he did not allow himself to be paralyzed by this disheartening prognosis. True to form, he would make the best of a difficult circumstance. One example of Dad's proactive initiative was helping to birth a Parkinson's support group. This group involvement was a radiant silver lining that highlighted the early sunset years of his life. While wrestling with his own disheartening limitations, Dad's focus became positively directed to serve others dealing with those same struggles. Mom was right by his side in this venture. Their commitment to serve others while coping with physical and emotional trials of their own was an inspiring witness to us.

Another major investment Dad made during those days was as a Gideon. Having nurtured a love for the scriptures over his lifetime, Dad discovered great delight in helping distribute Bibles to local schools, hospitals and hotels. The partnership with other Gideon couples provided an additional network of support and encouragement. As Dad's investment in music was diminishing, this Gideon involvement helped him cope with the deep sense of loss. Distributing Bibles probably reminded him of those prime-of-life experiences in Norristown, passing out gospel tracts door to door. The Gideon investment provided a welcome brightness to offset the increasing darkness of those sunset years.

* * *

"Are you ready to come to bed?" Dad asked Mom one evening. "I just have one box of dishes to pack. You can go awhile. I'll come soon," Mother replied. The previous weeks had been full of emotion-packed days as they sorted through years of accumulated possessions. Dad and Mom were preparing to move out of their home of fifty-five years to a small apartment at Dock Woods, a retirement center about five miles away.

The idea of moving had not been a welcome thought at first. Yet, it was obvious they could not manage the day-to-day upkeep of their large house and acre of property indefinitely. Dad's sister, Alice, was working as an interior decorator for the newly-built Dock Woods. Her input was significant in helping Dad and Mom come to terms with the advantages of retirement community living.

As Mom packed the last plate in the crammed box, she glanced around her kitchen. Thousands and thousands of hours had been spent in this room, preparing countless meals for her beloved family and treasured friends. Many times she had served her grandchildren around the kitchen table while the adults feasted in the dining room. Walking through the dining room and into the living room, the walls seemed to resonate with the hearty laughter, lively conversations, and music-making of days gone by. How could she leave this place with so many heart-stirring memories?

Completing the circle in Dad's office, she slowly mounted the stairs to their bedroom. Dad was already asleep when she quietly eased herself in next to him. As precious memories continued to stir her soul, tears found their way to her cheek. Gently she wiped them away. Mom wasn't accustomed to freely showing emotions. Her tears were often shed in secret and intimate feelings were usually hidden from those around her. Finally peaceful sleep came. Her faithful God of yesterday would be her faithful God of tomorrow.

After their move to Dock Woods, Dad continued to drive those five miles back and forth to the store. By this time, he was no longer able to play the guitar and teach. His ability to wait on customers had become quite labored. It was painful for us to observe Dad struggling to hang on to that which had been such a fulfilling part of his life. Harold had taken full ownership of the store several years earlier. The business was in good hands, and would prosper without him. Yet, Dad still felt an inner compulsion to hang on to his work. It was the only life he knew. There seemed to be no way we could convince him otherwise.

Approximately two months after their move, providence forced Dad's hand. A fall in the apartment caused by a blackout required him to be transferred to the skilled care unit there at Dock Woods. An apparent stroke, this setback was monumental. Regular therapy sessions helped Dad regain a bit of mobility. But he would never again drive or function independently. The sunset of his life was fast giving way to nightfall.

31

Blessings and Offerings

It was at this time that facing the imminent reality of Dad's death began confronting us. We continued to pray. A miracle healing was naturally our preferred choice. But, while reaching for a possible sovereign intervention, it also seemed wise to prepare ourselves for the termination of his life.

One of the considerations I [Wes] pondered was my desire to receive the intentional blessing of my father before his passing. From studying scriptural examples, I felt this expression of impartation from father to children was more significant than generally understood in our western culture. I sensed an increased longing for his words of blessing to be spoken over my life. I was somewhat intrigued by this desire stirring within, referencing it against my mixed feelings about Dad in earlier years.

During my late teen and early adult years, I sometimes wrestled against the obligation of being an extension of Dad and his music. I craved my own identity. The pioneering spirit in me would periodically rise up, urging me to cut my ties and move on to bigger and better and newer things. Playing the old hymns in Dad's band was often drudgery. I much preferred adding my creative touch to the new music of my day.

At no time did I ever openly despise my birthright, but I certainly had been guilty of devaluing it. Through the years, my perspective gradually changed. My unique heritage, previously taken for granted, was gradually becoming more precious. I found myself "tuning in" to the profound treasure of my Clemmer family destiny. Now, with the prospects of Dad's passing, I was intent on tapping its full potential. I wanted everything Dad had to give—not material things, but all that I was called to be as an extension of who he had become.

This desire for Dad's fatherly blessing was not solely for myself. I also coveted it for my siblings and their offspring. But in one sense, it seemed the window of opportunity had already passed. Generally, when visiting Dad, his speech was significantly hampered. We could catch only occasional words. It made dialog with him extremely difficult. How could this dream for a spoken pronouncement from Dad be realized? Thankfully, God is faithful to fulfill His ordained purposes. Providence prepared the way.

It was a bright, cheery day. I was alone, and had stopped by Dock Woods to visit with Dad. Not finding him in his room, I decided the likely place to search was the physical therapy department. Nearing the desk, I spotted Dad in his wheelchair, waiting for a transport person. After offering my services to the department clerk, I approached Dad. He looked up and spontaneously grinned, surprised to see me. After exchanging a few words of greeting, we headed for his room. As we turned the corner and moved down his corridor, I had a sudden burst of inspiration. We were approaching the doorway to a gathering room used for family visits and other group activities. "Hey Dad, let's sit here in the activity room rather than going back to your room," I proposed. Dad had a roommate, and this room was unoccupied. The sunny setting would provide a welcome change of scenery and also offer more privacy.

As I began inquiring about his day, I quickly noted that he seemed brighter and more articulate than normal. After a few more minutes of casual conversation, it suddenly dawned on me. This was the window of opportunity I had scarcely dared hope for. Dad was thinking clearly and speaking intelligibly. We were by ourselves, already enjoying the treasure of father-son interaction. I needed to seize the moment. It was destined to be a sacred one!

With a sense of expectancy, I launched into my "blessing" request. Dad listened intently and nodded occasionally as I referenced the biblical account of the patriarch, Jacob, speaking destiny over his sons. I

Dad passing on the family musical destiny to his oldest grandson, Scott, son of Wes.

then transitioned into personal commentary from my own heart. To begin, I expressed gratitude for his fathering role in my life. Dad's eyes began to moisten as I continued. "Dad, now that you are approaching the conclusion of your earthly assignment as my father, would you . . . would you pray your blessing over me?"

Without hesitation, Dad nodded. Reaching for my hand, he launched into a very simple but heart-stirring prayer of affirmation and blessing. Both of us were in tears as he uttered an emphatic "amen" to those spirit-directed words. It was a moment I shall never forget. There is no way to measure the value of that spiritual impartation.

* * *

Dock Woods could have been a wonderful place for Dad and Mom to conclude their life with us. But with Dad needing to remain in the extended care unit and Mom alone in her apartment, the arrangement was now less than ideal.

Harold, Lucy's husband, was the one who began voicing this concern most loudly. As a boy, Harold had vivid memories of his parents opening their home to care for aging parents. With this value instilled in him, Harold presented his proposal to the rest of us. If we agreed, he would build an in-law apartment onto their home next to the music store. This would enable Dad and Mom to live together with them. He and Lucy were also willing to be their primary caregivers. The entire family was in agreement, deeply appreciative of their sacrificial offer. What a wonderful God-honoring and parent-honoring solution.

After the construction was completed, we had the joy of moving Mom and Dad into their new apartment. It provided an ideal setting for their last days with us. Dad could sit in the sunroom of their apartment and keep tabs on the music store activity next door. Mom felt secure with her daughter close at hand, especially in the event of any emergency. It was also in this apartment setting we were destined to experience one of the ultimate blessings of Dad and Mom's entire sunset years.

In contrast to my spontaneous blessing encounter with Dad in the Dock Woods meeting room, this occasion for passing on the family blessing was planned. Siblings, spouses and grandchildren assembled around Mom and Dad in their apartment living room. After a brief word about the purpose for our gathering, each sibling and spouse, from eldest to youngest, presented themselves. Grandchildren were also included.

How precious as Dad and Mom prayed over us. By this time, Dad's voice was reduced to barely a whisper. We strained to catch enough words that would convey the heart of Dad as he spoke. Though a portion of what he prayed was unintelligible to our ears, we sensed the spirit behind those slurred words was imparting a blessing upon each family member. Generational affirmation and purpose was being passed on. The destiny of the Clemmer family was being intentionally extended!

* * *

As days passed, Dad continued to weaken. Finally, even his whispers were extinguished. Yet, one faint flicker of light remained. During our visits, I [Wes] frequently grabbed his guitar and started singing one of those familiar hymns so dear to his heart. Immediately, Dad would begin mouthing the words. Though the sound of his voice had ceased, the song in his heart was still very much alive. Dad's tongue was silent but his soul was singing. Oh, the power and God-radiating glory of spiritual song!

In the fall of 1996, Dad finally slipped into a coma. For several days we continued talking to him, sensing he was still able to hear. In the wee morning hours of October 23rd, Dad left us. As was declared about King David, Dad had fulfilled his purpose in his generation. Now he was in the presence of Christ, his redeemer and friend.

Mom let out a pitiful cry of anguish when she awakened, conscious of Dad's departure. Thankfully, he was now released from pain and enjoying the presence of God. But how could she go on without him? Mom knew that her days would be long and empty. Her distressed soul cried out to God for comfort and strength.

Dad's memorial service was held at the Franconia Mennonite Church on October 27th. How fitting, returning to the meeting house where his experience of congregational worship had begun. We returned to worship God, to comfort one another, to honor and remember Dad. And what is especially noteworthy, we siblings returned with a special sense of mission—to bring a unique offering of music. Finally, at Dad's memorial service, his music would be an acceptable offering in this house!

Throughout his pioneering years, Dad's unique expression of sacred instrumental music found acceptance and honor in far-away places around the globe. But that acceptance would never be expressed to Dad by the church family of his boyhood. Dad never experienced the fulfillment of that dream—playing his guitar and the music he loved at the Franconia meetinghouse. However, that dream was fulfilled by his sons and daughters. With our instruments and the gift of Dad's music, we began our offering presentation—with the familiar strains of Dad's theme song, "Have Thine Own Way Lord." What an honor to worship the Lord, filling the house with that sound. Dad's contribution as a musical pioneer was finally validated. His offering was acceptable. God was indeed having His way!

Mom's death followed only a few months later. Without the sense of responsibility to care for Dad, she quickly lost her will to live. We witnessed her life gradually ebbing away from her frail, weak body. It was difficult to see her experiencing excruciating physical pain during the last hours of her life.

In those final moments, we were gathered around her bed singing "God Be With You Till We Meet Again." Those words of blessing gently ushered her from this life into eternity. What a "welcome home" she must have experienced from Jesus and her beloved Joe.

Mother's memorial service was held at Towamencin Mennonite Church, February 6, 1997. As many paid tribute, it was noted her life and ministry reflected that of a "Mennonite Mother Theresa." Young and old remembered her expressions of encouragement with cards and letters, her gracious hospitality, her faithful prayers, and her positive attitude. Mom was committed to unity in the midst of opposing views. She certainly lived out one of her favorite verses. "If it be possible, as much as lieth in you, live at peace with all men."

It's not easy to say good-by to parents we love. But the precious memories and the impartation of their lives are the gifts that continue to live. Mom and Dad have left us a profound legacy. Their lives, poured out as offerings, have been translated into blessings impacting thousands upon thousands. May we be faithful in continuing to live and impart this legacy of offering and blessing for future generations—until Christ comes again!

Sons and daughters playing Dad's music during the memorial service held at the Franconia Mennonite meetinghouse, the church of his boyhood.

Children and spouses with Dad and Mom a few years before their death. Left to right, seated: Dean Clemmer, Ellen Clemmer, Dad, Jan Zeager, Charles Zeager. Standing: Lucy Gabman, Harold Gabman, Verna Clemmer, Wes Clemmer, Mom, Doris Stolzfus, Leonard Stolzfus.

Grandchildren and spouses with Dad and Mom a few years before their death. Left to right, seated: Rory Gabman (Kolb), Morr, Beth Zeager (Adams), Dad, Valerie Clemmer (Hall). Standing: Rochelle Gabman (Alderfer), Trish Zeager (Quinn), Roger Gabman, Bob Zeager, Rick Gabman, Doug Zeager, Scott Clemmer.

Epilogue

Tuning in to Family Destiny

God creates with a purpose. As He breathes life into each human soul, this lifeflow is not given simply to birth and sustain existence. His intention for us is abundant life—life with purposeful overflow. By yielding to the Spirit of God, men and women through the centuries have discovered and fulfilled their reason for being. It is by the Holy Spirit that persons are led to seek, uncover and ultimately fulfill divine destiny.

In God's original plan, parents have a primary role in helping children tune in to their destiny. To receive this insight, parents need a vital "tuned-in" connection with God, the Destiny Designer. Biblical stories vividly illustrate how this works. One intriguing example is the angelic visit with Joseph prior to the birth of his son, Jesus Christ. In this encounter, the angel revealed God's appointed calling upon Joseph's expected son.

Tuned in, Joseph heard these instructive words: "And she [Mary] will bear a son; and you [Joseph] shall call His name Jesus [Jah saves], for it is He who will save His people from their sins (Matt. 1:21 NASB)." As we can see, the name given to Jesus by his father represented more than what He was *to be called*. It also revealed what He was *called to be*. The significant point is this: Though He was Jesus Christ, it was important for the father [Joseph] to name him.

Another dimension of destiny discernment linked to the fathering factor is the family factor. In the Old Testament, God's people consisted of twelve tribes. This clan of families was known corporately as the Children of Israel. To them, family connections and ancestry were significant. Therefore, a person's purpose, while being expressed individually, was not to be fulfilled independently.

As with links in a chain, divine callings and destinies of individual persons require the dimension of corporate connection. If fulfilled according to God's intent, this perpetuates a multi-generational chain of blessing—blessing upon blessing, passed on from parent to child. In the true sense, to "bless" is to release and extend the potential of another.

Abraham is a prime example. His destiny as a leader-blesser and forefather of the ultimate Leader-Blesser was passed on to Isaac, his son. In turn, Isaac bestowed this blessing upon his son, Jacob. Before his death, Jacob called his sons together to declare what God showed him concerning their destinies. What he "named" over his son, Judah, is most revealing.

> *Judah, your brothers will praise you. You will grasp your enemies by the neck. All your relatives will bow before you. Judah, my son, is a young lion that has finished eating its prey. Like a lion he crouches and lies down; like a lioness—who dares to rouse him? The scepter will not depart from Judah, nor the ruler's staff from his descendants, until the coming of the one to whom it belongs, the one whom all nations will honor (Gen 49:9,10 NLT).*

Through this destiny-declaring prophecy, something was divinely released into future generations—a gifting of leadership potential. Judah's descendants would be graced to conquer and govern. History confirms the fulfillment of this fathering blessing. Judah's family produced many great and gifted leaders pre-dating the Messiah—the Ultimate Leader. David and Solomon are among the most renowned.

Naming and speaking destiny over generational offspring seems more familiar in biblical times. It was the father who helped the son to identify the purpose for which he was created. This calling of the son did not stand alone. It was vitally connected to the father—an extension of the family calling. These tuned-in fathers understood how important it was for the older generation to impart and extend family destiny to the younger up-and-coming generations.

In more recent times, the significance of family heritage in our culture has been grossly devalued. The broken family epidemic continues to spread. Deep woundedness inflicted by family triggers bitter alienation. Multitudes of children think pain rather than potential when contemplating what family has to offer. The family circle is broken.

Even in healthy, godly families, we are generally not educated to think in terms of family destiny. Typically, destiny is understood as an individual pursuit. Inheriting and extending God-designed potential bestowed through our roots is foreign to most. As responsible parents, we are highly motivated to provide material resourcing for our children. Yet, we often fail to comprehend the assignment of helping our offspring with this more crucial family destiny matter.

* * *

I doubt that Dad thought of pursuing family destiny while forming his first chords on that four-dollar Stella guitar. Playing instrumental music as a calling, especially within his rural Mennonite culture was unthinkable. To connect his budding love for the guitar with Pop's interest in the pump organ would have been a stretch. Pop played the organ more in earlier years. Later, the intriguing challenge of innovative farming pursuits sidelined most of his music-making. Raising sheep, bottling milk, harvesting the apple crop, and paying bills was the real deal. For Pop, music was a hobby for leisure, not a purpose to pursue. Men were called to work hard—not to play.

While playing the pump organ, Pop had little sense of what his interest in instrumental music might represent. He certainly didn't view it as an inheritance to pass on to his son, especially as a divine calling. Pop had no reference point. In the Mennonite culture of his day, any instrumental music-making was primarily for recreational enjoyment or a private expression of personal devotion—not a public expression of worship. Church music consisted of four-part acappella singing; a tradition highly revered and carefully guarded. The bishops and church leaders were insistent. Instrumental music-making in public religious gatherings was an old dispensation expression, reserved for the Old Testament era. Any sense of musical inheritance imparted from earlier Anabaptist generations would have been rooted in vocal music giftedness.

So it is understandable that Dad began tuning in to his musical destiny without recognizing the divine dialog of "deep calling unto deep." He did not have the benefit of a father like Jacob—a prophet's voice declaring destiny over his son. But without conscious realization, the still, small voice of prophetic utterance was being spoken over my Dad by his Pop. The fathering utterance was quietly speaking to the son through music, the language of the soul. It began to woo Dad in those early boyhood years. It whispered amid those throaty instrumental sounds of Pop's parlor reed organ. However, for the prophetic call to be clearly heard, another messenger was needed to awaken Dad to the discovery of his destiny.

For the prophetic word to be made more sure, the cowboy was sovereignly being moved into place. I'm sure Gotshall didn't look like a prophet or perceive himself to be a prophet. Nevertheless, he was one. God providentially purposed it to be so. But the medium of this prophet's word was not his *tongue*. It was his *tune*.

* * *

How intriguing. Dad tuned in to destiny through the tune of a non-relative—a cowboy! The limitation of Pop's prophetic shortsightedness was no limitation for God. As a master orchestrater of circumstances, the Master Conductor simply recruited someone from outside the family line to fill in the missing notes. It worked!

This is a profound lesson for us. When feeling shortchanged by life, we may tend to cast significant blame upon our imperfect parents. "If they had done it right, we could have gotten life right," is our rational line of defense. This faulty logic fails to take into account the faithfulness of God. When we (or our parents) are faithless, yet He remains faithful. But what might happen if you and I became faithful (intentional) in this matter? Now that's a thought!

There is clear evidence other relatives before Dad were stirred with a sense of fulfillment in making music. Though not officially documented, oral Clemmer family history notes a number of musicians from earlier generations. Unaware of their contributing role, they helped prepare the way for Dad.

Great-great-grandfather, Abraham M. Clemmer (1793-1879), had ten children. At least five of these ten exercised their musical gifting. Several were church song leaders. Another ancestor, Jacob Allebach

(1851-1909), tuned in to his musical destiny in a big way for that day. Jacob was an organist. In addition, he provided vocal and instrumental instruction, published music, and sold pump organs and pianos. I find it interesting that Dad never mentioned Jacob Allebach and the similarity of their vocations. The likely reason—Dad may never have heard of that fact. Thankfully, this was brought to our attention while putting together the pieces of this wonder-filled story.

Dad's destiny story. May it inspire our family and yours to be more intentional about multi-generational potential. Will you and your family purpose with us—to discover, to declare, and to fulfill what the Eternal Father has intended for our generation and those to come? What a privilege! What an opportunity! What a satisfaction!

Tuning in to family destiny. It's what we were created for. "For from Him and through Him and to Him are all things. To Him be the glory forever. Amen."

Appendix I

Creating a Memorial Stone
(Preserving Your Family Legacy)

The life of every person is a story worth telling. Each biography is a unique combination of hopes and dreams along with challenges and accomplishments. No matter how the ingredients are mixed, the history of persons, families, and nations are valuable life lessons to preserve. But these histories must be recorded if they are to enrich future generations.

It is especially beneficial to preserve personal family history. The priceless heritage of countless families is all but lost because no one has made the investment to record it. As mentioned in the foreword of this book, God places great importance on preserving memories for future generations. At various times in the scriptures, He inspired leaders to create monuments of remembrance. A monument is defined as "a lasting evidence or reminder of someone notable, a memorial stone erected in remembrance of a person."

Our journey of searching out and creating Dad and Mom's "memorial stone" has been a very rewarding experience. It is with this sense of fulfillment that we encourage you to consider recording the story of your parents as a witness for the future generations of your family. To preserve something is to value it—an expression of honor. Preserving the story of parents and forefathers is one practical way of fulfilling the biblical command to "honor your father and mother . . . that it may be well with you."

We trust that you will seriously consider making an investment to preserve your family legacy. Here are a few practical suggestions to help you begin.

Begin now. Don't wait until your parents are gone.

- Keep a journal of significant family happenings, many that take place in normal everyday life. Look for the extraordinary in the midst of the ordinary.
- Stay alert to the underlying significance (providential purposes) in special events. Happenings such as births, weddings, funerals, an unforeseen crisis or "mountain top" experience inevitably provoke deep feelings. Take advantage of these "golden moments" to explore what your parents are experiencing internally through the event. Record these findings in your journal along with the factual details so you have them for future reference when writing their story.
- Photographs are a great resource. Organizing photos in scrapbooks helps to preserve them for future reference. Including informative detail such as date, location, event, and the names of people is especially helpful.
- Family antiques, heirlooms, personal effects and souvenirs usually have intriguing stories behind them. Some of these items may even provide a vital connection to the stories of generations preceding your parents.

Enlist the help of others.

- **Your Parents (if they are living)** To begin the process, you may want to write a letter, expressing your gratitude for their investment in your life. As you communicate your intention to preserve their story in writing, invite them to participate with you. Use a video camera to reminisce with your parents. A series of questions can help direct the interaction towards subjects and experiences of special interest. The video and audio record of your parents will, in itself, be a priceless treasure gaining more value as the years pass.
- **Family Acquaintances (especially close friends)** Interviews with relatives and acquaintances were a great resource with our story. These friends contributed many colorful and valuable story pieces that we were missing. The same will be true for you. Each acquaintance offers their personal viewpoint developed over years

of interaction. The composite of additional perspectives will help provide a more complete and accurate picture of the main characters in your story.
- **Other Family Legacy Stories** Within the past several years, this idea of documenting and preserving family stories has become a more common practice. Reading the stories of others will help stir up creative ideas in you. This exposure can help you better decide how to proceed with your story.

Consider various formats.

- Your written legacy need not be published as a book. Begin by gathering pieces and allow the format to emerge. Some stories are quite simple and self-produced, consisting of several type-written pages stapled together. Others are published in a hard-bound book and sold commercially to the public. Many variations are possible. Any format is a worthwhile investment to preserve your family legacy.
- Determine how widely the story should be distributed. Is it primarily to be for the benefit of immediate family members? Does the story offer interest to an extended circle of people in the local community or even regions beyond? This consideration will have some bearing on the appropriate format to select for your project.

Look beyond the emerging story.

- The story in itself is a treasure, but there is more. God's purposes being fulfilled in and through our lives is what matters most. Allow the story to lead you to the reason for the story. There is multi-generational purpose and potential in your family just as there is in ours. Stay alert to the discovery of this. Remember, tuning in to family destiny is what the story is about!

Appendix II

Legacy Letter

June 23, 1992

Dear Dad,

How good to have you and Mom with us on Sunday. It seems like such a long time since you were here. I know the people at church were glad to see you again. Some had never met you before.

This morning, my thoughts were directed to you in a special way. Probably it had something to do with your visit on Sunday. I sensed something special beginning to stir then, but it really came together this morning. I decided to write my thoughts in a letter so you could read and reread it—to ponder and test it in your spirit.

I don't think I've ever written to you quite like this. It seems a bit odd, because through the years, I've always looked to you for advice and counsel. Some of what I'm about to share with you also relates to my present time of transition.

As you can imagine, it was quite difficult for me to think of turning Shiloh over to someone else. There have been times through the years when things were difficult with the church. In those seasons of struggle, I would have been glad to leave. But, I knew that wasn't the right response.

As I mentioned in the congregational letter, during the evaluation time of our recent sabbatical, it became clear I would be doing the church an injustice to continue on beyond what I was specifically called to do—establish the foundation. My primary focus these past few years has been to prepare a pastoral leader to build on that foundation. Even though it seems God is giving me the grace to let go, I know the real test will come in September when the transition is completed. The congregation has been so much of my life—and I still care. I want to see it succeed. To get on with what I feel I must share with you . . .

There is a truth I've been pondering for at least a year. It relates to how poorly most people pass on who they are and what God has done in their lives to the next generation. Remember how Moses exhorted the people to pass on to their sons the stories of what God had done so that the next generation wouldn't forget (Psalm 78:5-8). Each generation had a responsibility to impart to the next. I guess it's kinda like a chain. We need to be vitally connected to the link before us and the link after us if we are to really fulfill our purpose—what God has specifically called us to do.

I look at what God has done in your life. As I shared on Sunday, you effectively passed on to me the principles of tithing and missions. It would have been much more difficult for me to adopt these godly principles without you fulfilling your God-appointed duty as a father.

Also, in a very tangible way, you've passed on your music ministry to me and others in our family. Even though my generation is reshaping your contribution, it still represents destiny imparted by you. Some of us will carry it on more directly than others, but at least you were responsible to make it available.

Many times the "passing on" of family destiny happens in a very casual way. But, I believe the Lord has also purposed for impartation to be intentional. It relates to "the blessing" as passed on from one generation to the next—like Isaac, Jacob and others. This truth is not frequently taught. I believe we need to reconsider. I would challenge you, before you pass on, to consider imparting a prophetic blessing to each of your children. I know I personally desire to receive this from you.

As we begin asking the deeper questions about life, the Lord responds by revealing significant things we've been missing. It's easy to get so caught up in the lifestyle of the world, even as Christians, and not take advantage of the full potential assigned to us by God.

A few things from Sunday came to mind this morning as I read from Job 18:16,17,19. "His roots are dried below, and his branch is cut off above. Memory of him perishes from the earth and he has no name abroad. . . . He has no offspring or posterity among his people, nor any survivor where he sojourned."

The following is what I gleaned while I pondered this scripture:
- The ungodly live only for the now
- They fail to pour out—to impart—to the next generation
- Abundant life is the result of being vitally joined to our roots and to intentionally invest in our fruit (natural & spiritual sons & grandsons). A major part of our assignment as parents is to link the generations on either side of us.

How does all this relate to you? Well, I feel you have done some investing in us, the next generation. But I sensed as I considered more deeply, that the Lord would have you make another final contribution to your children and grandchildren. This further contribution could be as significant as those investments you've already made.

It has to do largely with your history. What made me think of it Sunday is when you shared a story from your growing-up years I had never heard before. In fact, I can't even remember now what it was. I think it had something to do with Uncle Jacob. Some of your stories I can remember because I've heard you tell them over and over. Once you are gone, these stories will become faint in my mind. Even more so, my children will have greater difficulty remembering them. These stories are part of what has made you who you are. Who you are is a vital part of what has made us [your children and grandchildren] who we are.

I think of the story you related again on Sunday—how the Lord miraculously gave you the chord-chart system of teaching guitar and accordion from the hymn book. What a powerful story. I told it in one of my teaching sessions in Guatemala and had to cry while sharing it with the missionaries. Yet, I'm sure I missed some of the details that could have made the recounting of it even more effective.

Dad, we need those and the countless other happenings recorded to help connect us to our roots. In this way, we can also be more effective in connecting the next generations. So many children today have almost no sense of their roots. Therefore, they struggle to connect with who they are called to be.

I didn't see the importance of this in earlier years. All I was concerned about was my life, my wants, etc. Even in my ministry, I see my main calling now is to impart what God has imparted to me. My primary work is to intentionally pass on who I am to my children, both spiritual and physical. Fathers and mothers are going to their death bed failing to see this God-ordained responsibility. They have been too busy fulfilling their own pursuits, however good they may be.

I would like to throw out something for you to consider. I know this may be difficult for you to think about. It means letting go of something very dear to you, just like the Shiloh pastorate has been for me. I see your work at the store draining away time and energy that could be spent leaving an intentional legacy for those of us following in your shoes. I remember hearing your comment about some people who suggested you stop working at the store. That might be a bit radical. But I suggest that you consider reducing your hours—working a few days each week.

No, I'm not proposing that you sit at home and do nothing. Instead, you and Mom could take the time to write down all the life stories you can think of from your past. As you recount them, she could write. I would also like to use my video camera to photograph some of the stories as well.

I know it would be a lot of work for you, and not the kind familiar to you. It's easier to go to the store as you've done for years rather than write your stories. You don't view yourself as a storyteller. You identify yourself as a musician and businessman. But, the fact is, you are a storyteller too. People have loved your stories for years. Could it be that God developed this gift to prepare you for a final season of storytelling—to record for future generations what would otherwise be lost?

This is a radical proposal, and I debated whether or not to share it. I was afraid you would misunderstand or think I was speaking out of turn. Yet, I could not shake what I sensed and needed to be obedient.

I would like to talk in more detail about it sometime after you pray and consider what I've written. The Holy Spirit must give you an inner witness. I just read last week that Billy Graham is intending to significantly reduce his crusade schedule to work on his memoirs with

Cliff Barrows, George Beverly Shea, Grady Wilson and other associates. He must be sensing a similar challenge from God.

Dad, I love you very, very much. Words will never describe the gratitude in my heart as I consider what you have already imparted to me. It seems almost selfish to ask more of you in these sunset years. But, my heart desire is to be responsible in passing on to my natural and spiritual children the blessing of the Lord which has come down through the generations. We indeed have a rich heritage. "Our lines have fallen in pleasant places . . ."

God's best to you and Mother.

Your Son,
Wes

Appendix III

Chord Chart and Theme Song

Though not formally trained, Dad was inspired to develop a method enabling guitarists to play chords with hymns. This involves identifying accented beats of the song. On those beats, the soprano, alto, tenor and bass notes generally point to an identifiable chord which is then handwritten above the musical staff. Both this chart and the chords written in the accompanying theme song, "Have Thine Own Way, Lord" are in Dad's handwriting.

Key of C
C = C - E - G
F = F - A - C
G7 = G - B - D - F

Key of G = 1 Sharp
G = G - B - D
C = C - E - G
D7 = D - F# - A - C

Key of D = 2 Sharps
D = D - F# - A
G = G - B - D
A7 = A - C# - E - G

Key of A = 3 Sharps
A = A - C# - E
D = D - F# - A
E7 = E - G# - B - D

Key of E = 4 Sharps
E = E - G# - B
A = A - C# - E
B7 = B - D# - F# - A

C - 3 - D *Key of F = 1 flat*
F = F - A - C
Bb = Bb - D - F
C7 = C - E - G - Bb

C - 3 - G *Key of Bb = 2 flats*
Bb = Bb - D - F
Eb = Eb - G - Bb
F7 = F - A - C - Eb

C - 1 - D *Key of Eb = 3 flats*
Eb = Eb - G - Bb
Ab = Ab - C - Eb
Bb7 = Bb - D - F - Ab

C - 1 - G *Key of Ab = 4 flats*
Ab = Ab - C - Eb
Db = Db - F - Ab
Eb7 = Eb - G - Bb - Db

C - 2 - G

C - 2 - D

C - 1 - C *Key of Db = 5 flats*
Db = Db - F - Ab
Gb = Gb - Bb - D
Ab7 = Ab - C - E - Gb